THE INTIMATE ENEMY

THE INTIMATE ENEMY

Loss and Recovery of Self
under Colonialism

ASHIS NANDY

OXFORD
UNIVERSITY PRESS

OXFORD
UNIVERSITY PRESS

YMCA Library Building, Jai Singh Road, New Delhi 110 001

Oxford University Press is a department of the University of Oxford. It furthers the
University's objective of excellence in research, scholarship, and education
by publishing worldwide in

Oxford   New York

Auckland   Cape Town   Dar es Salaam   Hong Kong   Karachi   Kuala Lumpur
Madrid   Melbourne   Mexico City   Nairobi   New Delhi   Shanghai   Taipei   Toronto

With offices in

Argentina   Austria   Brazil   Chile   Czech Republic   France   Greece   Guatemala
Hungary   Italy   Japan   Poland   Portugal   Singapore   South Korea   Switzerland
Thailand   Turkey   Ukraine   Vietnam

Oxford is a registered trademark of Oxford University Press
in the UK and in certain other countries

Published in India by Oxford University Press, New Delhi

First published 1983
Oxford India Paperbacks 1988
Twenty-fifth impression 2009

ISBN-13: 978-0-19-562237-9
ISBN-10: 0-19-562237-5

Printed in India by Sai Print-O-Pack Pvt. Ltd., New Delhi 110 020
Published by Oxford University Press
YMCA Library Building, Jai Singh Road, New Delhi 110 001

To
Prafulla Nalini Nandy
and Sarala Nandy

Contents

Preface

'Through a curious transposition peculiar to our times', Albert Camus once wrote, 'it is innocence that is called upon to justify itself.' The two essays here justify and defend the innocence which confronted modern Western colonialism and its various psychological offshoots in India.

Modern colonialism won its great victories not so much through its military and technological prowess as through its ability to create secular hierarchies incompatible with the traditional order. These hierarchies opened up new vistas for many, particularly for those exploited or cornered within the traditional order. To them the new order looked like—and here lay its psychological pull—the first step towards a more just and equal world. That was why some of the finest critical minds in Europe—and in the East—were to feel that colonialism, by introducing modern structures into the barbaric world, would open up the non-West to the modern critical-analytic spirit. Like the 'hideous heathen god who refused to drink nectar except from the skulls of murdered men', Karl Marx felt, history would produce out of oppression, violence and cultural dislocation not merely new technological and social forces but also a new social consciousness in Asia and Africa. It would be critical in the sense in which the Western tradition of social criticism—from Vico to Marx—had been critical and it would be rational in the sense in which post-Cartesian Europe had been rational. It is thus that the ahistorical primitives would one day, the expectation went, learn to see themselves as masters of nature and, hence, as masters of their own fate.

Many many decades later, in the aftermath of that marvel of modern technology called the Second World War and perhaps that modern encounter of cultures called Vietnam, it has become obvious that the drive for mastery over men is not merely a by-product of a faulty political economy but also of a world view which believes in the absolute superiority of the human over the nonhuman and the subhuman, the masculine over the feminine, the adult over the child, the historical over the ahistorical, and the modern or progressive over the traditional or the savage. It has become more and more apparent that genocides, ecodisasters and ethnocides are but the underside of corrupt sciences and psychopathic technologies wedded to new secular hierarchies, which have reduced major civilizations to the status of a set of empty rituals. The ancient forces of human greed and violence, one recognizes, have merely found a new legitimacy in anthropocentric doctrines of secular salvation, in the ideologies of progress, normality and hyper-masculinity, and in theories of cumulative growth of science and technology.

This awareness has not made everyone give up his theory of progress but it has given confidence to a few to look askance at the old universalism within which the earlier critiques of colonialism were offered. It is now possible for some to combine fundamental social criticism with a defence of non-modern cultures and traditions. It is possible to speak of the plurality of critical traditions and of human rationality. At long last we seem to have recognized that neither is Descartes the last word on reason nor is Marx that on the critical spirit.

The awareness has come at a time when the attack on the non-modern cultures has become a threat to their survival. As this century with its bloodstained record draws to a close, the nineteenth century dream of one world has re-emerged, this time as a nightmare. It haunts us with the prospect of a fully homogenized, technologically controlled, absolutely hierarchized world, defined by polarities like the modern and the primitive, the secular and the non-secular, the scientific and the unscientific, the expert and the layman, the normal and the abnormal, the developed and the underdeveloped, the vanguard and the led, the liberated and the savable.

This idea of a brave new world was first tried out in the colonies. Its carriers were people who, unlike the rapacious first generation of bandit-kings who conquered the colonies, sought to be helpful. They were well-meaning, hard-working, middle-class missionaries, liberals, modernists, and believers in science, equality and progress. The bandit-kings, presumably like bandit-kings everywhere, robbed, maimed and killed; but sometimes they did so without a civilizing mission and mostly with only crude concepts of racism and *untermensch*. They faced —and expected to face—other civilizations with their versions of middle kingdoms and barbarians; the pure and the impure; the *kafirs* and the *moshreks*; and the *yavanas* and the *mlecchas*. However vulgar, cruel or stupid it might have once been, that racism now faces defeat. It is now time to turn to the second form of colonization, tne one which at least six generations of the Third World have learnt to view as a prerequisite for their liberation. This colonialism colonizes minds in addition to bodies and it releases forces within the colonized societies to alter their cultural priorities once for all. In the process, it helps generalize the concept of the modern West from a geographical and temporal entity to a psychological category. The West is now everywhere, within the West and outside; in structures and in minds.

This is primarily the story of the second colonization and resistances to it. That is why these essays are also forays into contemporary politics; after all, we are concerned with a colonialism which survives the demise of empires. At one time, the second colonization legitimized the first. Now, it is independent of its roots. Even those who battle the first colonialism often guiltily embrace the second. Hence the reader should read the following pages not as history but as a cautionary tale. They caution us that conventional anti-colonialism, too, could be an apologia for the colonization of minds. If the following account displays a 'distorted' view of some of the Enlightenment figures and of radical social critics in Europe, it is a part of the same story. They do not often look the same when the viewpoint is the immediacy of the new oppression and the possibility of cultural defeat. Nor have I, for the same reason, managed to make some well-known reactionaries look as villainous as many would have liked. Time has rendered them either toothless or unwitting allies of the victims.

This book takes the idea of psychological resistance to colonialism seriously. But that implies some new responsibilities, too. Today, when 'Westernization' has become a pejorative word, there have reappeared on the stage subtler and more sophisticated means of acculturation. They produce not merely models of conformity but also models of 'official' dissent. It is possible today to be anti-colonial in a way which is specified and promoted by the modern world view as 'proper', 'sane' and 'rational'. Even when in opposition, that dissent remains predictable and controlled. It is also possible today to opt for a non-West which itself is a construction of the West. One can then choose between being the Orientalist's despot, to combine Karl Wittfogel with Edward Said, and the revolutionary's loving subject, to combine Camus with George Orwell. And for those who do not like the choice, there is, of course, Cecil Rhodes' and Rudyard Kipling's noble, half-savage half-child, compared to whom the much-hated Brown Sahib seems more brown than sahib. Even in enmity these choices remain forms of homage to the victors. Let us not forget that the most violent denunciation of the West produced by Frantz Fanon is written in the elegant style of a Jean-Paul Sartre. The West has not merely produced modern colonialism, it informs most interpretations of colonialism. It colours even this interpretation of interpretation.

I have said at the beginning that these pages justify innocence. This statement should be amplified in a world where the rhetoric of progress uses the fact of internal colonialism to subvert the cultures of societies subject to external colonialism and where the internal colonialism in turn uses the fact of external threat to legitimize and perpetuate itself. (It is however also a world where the awareness has grown that neither form of oppression can be eliminated without eliminating the other.) In the following pages I have in mind something like the 'authentic innocence' psychoanalyst Rollo May speaks about, the innocence which includes the vulnerability of a child but which has not lost the realism of its perception of evil or that of its own 'complicity' with that evil. It was that innocence which finally defeated colonialism, however much the modern mind might like to give the credit to world historical forces, internal contradictions of capitalism and to the political horse-sense or 'voluntary self-liquidation' of the rulers.

But the meek inherit the earth not by meekness alone. They have to have categories, concepts and, even, defences of mind with which to turn the West into a reasonably manageable vector within the traditional world views still outside the span of modern ideas of universalism. The first concept in such a set has to be the victims' construction of the West, a West which would make sense to the non-West in terms of the non-West's experience of suffering. However jejune such a concept may seem to the sophisticated scholar, it is a reality for the millions who have learnt the hard way to live with the West during the last two centuries.

And, everything said, that alternative construction of the West is not so unsophisticated after all. If there is the non-West which constantly invites one to be Western and to defeat the West on the strength of one's acquired Westernness—there is the non-West's construction of the West which invites one to be true to the West's other self and to the non-West which is in alliance with that other self. If beating the West at its own game is the preferred means of handling the feelings of self-hatred in the modernized non-West, there is also the West constructed by the savage outsider who is neither willing to be a player nor a counterplayer. Those other Wests, too, I have tried to capture in these pages. In this connection if, while translating and commenting on their Wests, these outsiders have smuggled in their own imageries, myths and fantasies, I have connived at it; that is the way translations and commentaries are tradi-tionally made in some societies. Fidelity to one's inner self, as one translates, and to one's inner voice, when one comments, may not mean adherence to reality in some cultures but in some others they do. At least that is the sole defence I have for my tendency to speak of the West as a single political entity, of Hinduism as Indianness, or of history and Christianity as Western. None of them is true but all of them are realities. I like to believe that each such concept in this work is a *double entendre*: on the one hand, it is a part of an oppressive structure; on the other, it is in league with its victims. Thus, the West is not merely a part of an imperial world view; its classical traditions and its critical self are sometimes a protest against the modern West. Similarly, Hinduism is Indianness the way V. S. Naipaul speaks of it; and Hinduism could be Indianness the way Rabindranath Tagore actualized it. At one time these could be ignored as trivialities. Today, these differences have become clues to survival. Especially so when the modern West has produced not only its servile imitators and admirers but also its circus-tamed opponents and its tragic counterplayers performing their last gladiator-like acts of courage in front of appreciative Caesars. The essays in this book are a paean to the non-players, who construct a West which allows them to live with the alternative West, while resisting the loving embrace of the West's dominant self.

Thus, the colonized Indians do not remain in these pages simple-hearted victims of colonialism; they become participants in a moral and cognitive venture against oppression. They make choices. And to the extent they have chosen their alternative within the West, they have also evaluated the evidence, judged, and sentenced some while acquitting others. For all we know, the Occident may survive as a civilization partly as a result of this ongoing revaluation, perhaps to an extent even outside the geographical perimeters of the West. On the other hand, the standard opponents of the West, the counterplayers, are not, in spite of their vicious rhetoric, outside the dominant model of universalism. They have been integrated within the dominant consciousness—type-cast, if you like—as ornamental dissenters. I suspect that the universalism of those 'simple' outsiders, the non-players who have been the victims of modernity—the armed version of which is sometimes called colonialism—is a higher-order universalism than the ones popularized during the last two centuries.

I do not therefore hesitate to declare these essays to be an alternative mythography of history which denies and defies the values of history. I hope the essays capture in the process something of the ordinary Indian's psychology of colonialism. I reject the model of the gullible, hopeless victim of colonialism caught in the hinges of history. I see him as fighting his own battle for survival in his own way, sometimes consciously, sometimes by default. I have only sought to clarify his assumptions and his world view in all their self-contradictory richness. That way may not be our idea of what a proper battle against colonialism ought to be like. But I doubt if he cares.

This is why in the second essay even the babu has been grudgingly recognized as an interface who processes the West on behalf of his society and reduces it to a digestible bolus. Both his comical and dangerous selves protect his society against the White Sahib. And even that White Sahib may turn out to be defined, not by skin colour, but by social and political choices. Certainly he turns out to be, in these pages, not the conspiratorial dedicated oppressor that he is made out to be, but a self-destructive co-victim with a reified life style and a parochial culture, caught in the hinges of history he swears by. In the age of Adolf Eichmann, one might add, a Rudyard Kipling can only hope to be an unheroic foot soldier and supply cannon fodder. All theories of salvation, secular or non-secular, which fail to understand this degradation of the colonizer are theories which indirectly admit the superiority of the oppressors and collaborate with them.

The essential reasoning is simple. Between the modern master and the non-modern slave, one must choose the slave not because one should choose voluntary poverty or admit the superiority of suffering, not only because the slave is oppressed, not even because he works (which, Marx said, made him less alienated than the master). One must choose the slave also because he represents a higher-order cognition which perforce

includes the master as a human, whereas the master's cognition
has to exclude the slave except as a 'thing'. Ultimately, modern
oppression, as opposed to the traditional oppression, is not an
encounter between the self and the enemy, the rulers and the
ruled, or the gods and the demons. It is a battle between de-
humanized self and the objectified enemy, the technologized
bureaucrat and his reified victim, pseudo-rulers and their fear-
some other selves projected on to their 'subjects'.

That is the difference between the Crusades and Auschwitz,
between Hindu–Muslim riots and modern warfare. That is
why the following pages speak only of victims; when they
speak of victors, the victors are ultimately shown to be camou-
flaged victims, at an advanced stage of psychosocial decay.

This work is primarily an enquiry into the psychological structures and cultural forces which supported or resisted the culture
of colonialism in British India. But it also is, by implication, a
study of post-colonial consciousness. It deals with elements of
Indian traditions which have emerged less innocent from the
colonial experience and it deals with cultural and psychological strategies which have helped the society to survive the
experience with a minimal defensive redefinition of its selfhood
For parts of the book, therefore, colonialism in India began in
1757, when the battle of Plassey was lost by the Indians, and it
ended in 1947, when the British formally withdrew from the
country; for other parts of the book, colonialism began in the
late 1820s when policies congruent with a colonial theory of
culture were first implemented and it ended in the 1930s when
Gandhi broke the back of the theory; for still other parts of the
book colonialism began in 1947, when the outer supports to
the colonial culture ended, and resistance to it is still continuing.

It goes without saying that I have not tried to give a complete
picture of the Indian mind under colonialism. I have selected
my examples and chosen my informants, to make some rather
specific points. These points are political. Their referents lie
in the realm of public politics as well as in the politics of cultures
and cultural knowledge. And at both planes, they get involved

in the politics of the modern categories usually employed to analyse man-made suffering. The unstated assumption is that an ethically sensitive and culturally rooted alternative social knowledge is already partly available outside the modern social sciences—in those who have been the 'subjects', consumers or experimentees of these sciences. There are two colonialisms in these pages, and subjecthood to one is examined with an awareness of the subjecthood to the other.

This framework explains the partial, almost cavalier, use of the biographical data and the deliberate misuse of some concepts borrowed from modern psychology and sociology. The aim is not to adjust, alter or refurbish Indian experiences to fit the existing psychological and social theories—to make a better case for cultural relativism or for a more relativist cross-cultural psychology. The aim is to make sense of some of the relevant categories of contemporary knowledge in Indian terms and put them in a competing theory of universalism. What the subjects of Western colonialism did unselfconsciously, I am trying to do consciously and without being able to fully shed my professional baggage. The colonized Indians did not always try to correct or extend the Orientalists; in their own diffused way, they tried to create an alternative language of discourse. This was their anti-colonialism; it is possible to make it ours, too. At one place in this book I use the example of Iswar Chandra Vidyasagar (1820–91) who, though deeply impressed by Western rationalist thought and though himself an agnostic, lived like an orthodox pandit and formulated his dissent in indigenous terms. He did not counterpoise John Locke or David Hume against *Manusaṁhitā*; he counterpoised the *Parāśara Sūtra*. This was his way of handling not only Indian social problems but also the exogenous idea of rationalism. (I believe, perhaps wrongly, that rationalism too could learn something from this odd version of it.) It is the second part of the story— an unheroic but critical traditionalism which develops a sensitivity to new experiences of evil—which I have stressed. Even if this sounds hopelessly like another case of unresolved 'counter-transference', I hope this book contributes to that stream of critical consciousness: the tradition of reinterpretation of traditions to create new traditions.

Admittedly I have, in the following pages, picked up clues from—and quarrels with—contemporary social sciences. But my dialogue or debate is mainly with those who have shaped and are shaping the Indian consciousness, not so much with the world of professional social sciences. Modern colonialism is too serious a matter to be left entirely to the latter.

For those who are not happy unless they know the element of self-interest in any methodology—I count myself among them—this approach *does* give me a distinct and rather unfair advantage. I suspect that a purely professional critique of this book will not do. If you do not like it, you will have to fight it the way one fights myths: by building or resurrecting more convincing myths.

However, even myths have their biases. Let me state some of those associated with mine. In the following pages, I have deliberately focused on the living traditions, emphasizing the dialectic between the classical, the pure and the high-status on the one hand, and the folksy, hybrid and the low-brow on the other. As I have already said, it is the unheroic Indian coping with the might of the West I want to portray. To him, the classical and the folk, the pure and the hybrid, are all parts of a larger repertoire. He uses them impartially in the battle of minds in post-colonial India.

Secondly, a comment about the more academic concerns called psychological anthropology and Freudian social psychology with which I have maintained a close relationship for two decades and from which this book, if written even five years ago, would have borrowed much of its theoretical frame. There is a clear tradition in works of this kind and one must state in what way this book deviates from that tradition. I have *not* tried to interpret here Indian personality or culture and to show their fate under colonial rule according to any fixed concept of health, native or exogenous. Instead, I have presumed certain continuities between personality and culture and seen in them political and ethical possibilities. These possibilities are sometimes accepted and sometimes not. In other words, I have tried to retain the critical edge of depth psychology but shifted the locus of criticism from the purely psychological to the psycho-political. There is in these pages an attempt to demystify conventional psychological techniques of demystification, too.

This however means that the broad empirical outline of Indian personality has been taken for granted by me. In the last twenty-five years, a galaxy of psychiatrists, psychoanalysts, anthropologists, philosophers and even political economists have studied the various dimensions of the Indian mind. This knowledge is now a part of the Indian self-image. One should be able to build upon it. Thus, I have not discussed many aspects of Indian selfhood which would have given a touch of completeness to the following analysis. Nor have I done full justice to the individual witnesses I have called from the past to argue my case or to the textual traditions I have invoked. In this respect, I am guilty of leaving a number of loose ends which will have to be tied up by the fastidious reader, either with the help of his superior knowledge of the Indian mind and culture or by his intuitive understanding of them. I hope nevertheless to have provided clues to *one* possible meaning of living in this civilization *today*. To the extent I have succeeded in freeing that meaning from the shackles of cultural relativism and managed to restore to it its claim to an alternative universality, the following interpretation of Indian traditions will not have been in vain and it will have some relevance for other cultures under attack. After all, this work is based on the assumption that all man-made suffering is one and everyone has a responsibility.

Finally, a word on the possible 'sexism' of my language. This issue has dogged my steps for a while and I want to state my position on it once for all. English is not my language. Though I have developed a taste for it, it was once forced upon me. Even now I often form my thoughts in my native Bengali and then translate when I have to put them down on paper. Now that after thirty years of toil I have acquired reasonable competence in the language, I am told by the progeny of those who first imposed it on me that I have been taught the wrong English by their forefathers; that I must now relearn the language. Frankly, I am too old to do so. Those who are offended by my language may console themselves by remembering that the language in which I think has traditionally looked at the male and the female differently.

Parts of an earlier version of 'The Psychology of Colonialism' were published in *Psychiatry*, 1982, 45(3). It was written in response to an invitation from the Indian Council of Social Science Research which provided some financial support too. The paper has benefited from the detailed criticisms and suggestions given by André Béteille, Manoranjan Mahanty, Sumit and Tanika Sarkar, Kenichi Nakamura, W. H. Morris-Jones and Veena Das.

The 'Uncolonized Mind' has grown out of a presentation I made at a meeting on Culture, Power and Transformation, organized by the World Order Models Project at Poona in July 1978. Parts of an earlier version of it were published in the *Times of India*, October 1978 and in *Alternatives*, 1982, 8(1). The present version has gained much from comments and suggestions from M. P. Sinha, Giri Deshingkar, Girdhar Rathi and R. A. P. Shastri. The preface draws upon an article published in the *Times of India*, February 1983.

M. K. Riyal and Bhuvan Chandra have prepared the manuscript, Sujit Deb and Tarun Sharma have given bibliographic help. Without my wife Uma and my daughter Aditi I would have finished the work earlier but it would not have been the same.

One

The Psychology of Colonialism: Sex, Age and Ideology in British India

I

Imperialism was a sentiment rather than a policy; its foundations were moral rather than intellectual . . .

D. C. Somervell[1]

It is becoming increasingly obvious that colonialism—as we have come to know it during the last two hundred years— cannot be identified with only economic gain and political power. In Manchuria, Japan consistently lost money, and for many years colonial Indochina, Algeria and Angola, instead of increasing the political power of France and Portugal, sapped it. This did not make Manchuria, Indochina, Algeria or Angola less of a colony. Nor did it disprove that economic gain and political power are important *motives* for creating a colonial situation. It only showed that colonialism could be characterized by the search for economic and political advantage without concomitant *real* economic or political gains, and sometimes even with economic or political losses.[2]

This essay argues that the first differentia of colonialism is a state of mind in the colonizers and the colonized, a colonial consciousness which includes the sometimes unrealizable wish to make economic and political profits from the colonies, but

---

[1] *English Thought in the Nineteenth Century* (New York: Longman Green, 1929), p. 186.

[2] I am for the moment ignoring the fact that the colonial societies in our times lost out in the game of political and economic power in the First World itself.

other elements too. The political economy of colonization is of course important, but the crudity and inanity of colonialism are principally expressed in the sphere of psychology and, to the extent the variables used to describe the states of mind under colonialism have themselves become politicized since the entry of modern colonialism on the world scene, in the sphere of political psychology. The following pages will explore some of these psychological contours of colonialism in the rulers and the ruled and try to define colonialism as a shared culture which may not always begin with the establishment of alien rule in a society and end with the departure of the alien rulers from the colony. The example I shall use will be that of India, where a colonial political economy began to operate seventy-five years before the full-blown ideology of British imperialism became dominant, and where thirty-five years after the formal ending of the Raj, the ideology of colonialism is still triumphant in many sectors of life.

Such disjunctions between politics and culture became possible because it is only partly true that a colonial situation produces a theory of imperialism to justify itself. Colonialism is also a psychological state rooted in earlier forms of social consciousness in both the colonizers and the colonized. It represents a certain cultural continuity and carries a certain cultural baggage.

First, it includes codes which both the rulers and the ruled can share. The main function of these codes is to alter the original cultural priorities on both sides and bring to the centre of the colonial culture subcultures previously recessive or subordinate in the two confronting cultures. Concurrently, the codes remove from the centre of each of the cultures subcultures previously salient in them. It is these fresh priorities which explain why some of the most impressive colonial systems have been built by societies ideologically committed to open political systems, liberalism and intellectual pluralism. That this split parallels a basic contradiction within the modern scientific-rational world view which, while trying to remain rational within its confines, has consistently refused to be rational *vis-*

à-vis other traditions of knowledge after acquiring world dominance, is only the other side of the same explanation.[3] It also
explains why colonialism never seems to end with formal political freedom. As a state of mind, colonialism is an indigenous
process released by external forces. Its sources lie deep in the
minds of the rulers and the ruled. Perhaps that which begins in
the minds of men must also end in the minds of men.

Second, the culture of colonialism presumes a particular
style of managing dissent. Obviously, a colonial system per-
petuates itself by inducing the colonized, through socio-
economic and psychological rewards and punishments, to accept new social norms and cognitive categories. But these outer
incentives and dis-incentives are invariably noticed and challenged; they become the overt indicators of oppression and
dominance. More dangerous and permanent are the inner
rewards and punishments, the secondary psychological gains
and losses from suffering and submission under colonialism.
They are almost always unconscious and almost always ignored.
Particularly strong is the inner resistance to recognizing the
ultimate violence which colonialism does to its victims, namely
that it creates a culture in which the ruled are constantly
tempted to fight their rulers within the psychological limits set
by the latter. It is not an accident that the specific variants of
the concepts with which many anti-colonial movements in our
times have worked have often been the products of the imperial
culture itself and, even in opposition, these movements have
paid homage to their respective cultural origins. I have in mind
not only the overt Apollonian codes of Western liberalism that
have often motivated the élites of the colonized societies but
also their covert Dionysian counterparts in the concepts of

[3] On this other contradiction see Paul Feyerabend, *Science in a Free Society*
(London: NLB, 1978). In the context of India and China this point emerges
clearly from Claude Alvares' *Homo Faber: Technology and Culture in India, China and
the West, 1500–1972* (New Delhi: Allied Publishers, 1979). See also Ashis Nandy,
'Science, Authoritarianism and Culture: On the Scope and Limits of Isolation
outside the Clinic', M. N. Roy Memorial Lecture, 1980, *Seminar*, May 1981 (261);
and Shiv Viswanathan, 'Science and the Sense of Other', paper written for the
colloquium on New Ideologies for Science and Technology, Lokayan Project 1982,
Delhi, mimeographed.

statecraft, everyday politics, effective political methods and utopias which have guided revolutionary movements against colonialism.

The rest of this essay examines, in the context of these two processes and as illustrations, how the colonial ideology in British India was built on the cultural meanings of two fundamental categories of institutional discrimination in Britain, sex and age, and how these meanings confronted their traditional Indian counterparts and their new incarnations in Gandhi.

II

The homology between sexual and political dominance which Western colonialism invariably used—in Asia, Africa and Latin America—was not an accidental by-product of colonial history. It had its correlates in other situations of oppression with which the West was involved, the American experience with slavery being the best documented of them. The homology, drawing support from the denial of psychological bisexuality in men in large areas of Western culture, beautifully legitimized Europe's post-medieval models of dominance, exploitation and cruelty as natural and valid. Colonialism, too, was congruent with the existing Western sexual stereotypes and the philosophy of life which they represented. It produced a cultural consensus in which political and socio-economic dominance symbolized the dominance of men and masculinity over women and femininity.

During the early years of British rule in India, roughly between 1757 and 1830, when the British middle classes were not dominant in the ruling culture and the rulers came mainly from a feudal background, the homology between sexual and political dominance was not central to the colonial culture.[4] Most

---

[4] Frantz Fanon was one of the first to point out the psychological dominance of the European middle-class culture in the colonies. See his *Black Skin, White Masks* translated by C. L. Markman (New York: Grove, 1967); also Gustav Jahoda, *White Man* (London: Oxford University Press, 1961), pp. 102, 123. Quoted in Renate Zahar, *Frantz Fanon: Colonialism and Alienation* (New York: Monthly Review Press, 1974), p. 45n. James Morris (*Pax Britannica's Command: An Imperial Progress*, London: Faber and Faber, 1973, p. 38) says, in the context of India: 'By 1835 one

rulers and subjects had not yet internalized the idea of colonial rule as a manly or husbandly or lordly prerogative. I am not speaking here of the micro-politics of colonialism but of its macro-politics. Individual racialists and sadists were there aplenty among the British in India. But while British rule had already been established, British culture in India was still not politically dominant, and race-based evolutionism was still inconspicuous in the ruling culture. Most Britons in India lived like Indians at home and in the office, wore Indian dress, and observed Indian customs and religious practices. A large number of them married Indian women, offered *pūjā* to Indian gods and goddesses, and lived in fear and awe of the magical powers of the Brāhmaṇs. The first two governor-generals, renowned for their rapaciousness, were also known for their commitment to things Indian. Under them, the traditional Indian life style dominated the culture of British Indian politics. Even the British Indian Army occasionally had to pay respect to Indian gods and goddesses and there was at least one instance when the army made money from the revenues of a temple. Finally, missionary activity in British India was banned, Indian laws dominated the courts and the system of education was Indian.[5]

In Britain, too, the idea of empire was suspect till as late as the 1830s. Visitors to colonies like India often found the British authority there 'faintly comical'.[6] The gentlemen of the East

---

detects a certain smugness among the islanders, and this superior tone of voice came not as it would later come, from an arrogant Right, but from a highly moralistic Left. The middle classes, newly enfranchised, were emerging into power: and it was the middle classes who would eventually prove, later in Victoria's reign, the most passionate imperialists of all.'

It is in the context of this correlation between middle class culture and the spirit of imperialism that one must make sense of psychologist J. D. Unwin's reported proposition: 'only a sexually restrained society . . . would continue to expand' (*Heaven's Command*, p. 30). The political culture of British India was however a product of the dialectic between British feudalism and British middle class culture. I have avoided the details of this dialectic here.

[5] E.g., Harihar Sheth, *Prācīn Kalikātār Pariċay* (Calcutta: Orient Book, 1982), new ed; Binoy Ghose, *Kalkātā Culture* (Calcutta: Bihar Sahitya Bhavan, 1953); Morris, *Heaven's Command*, pp. 75–6.

[6] Morris, *Heaven's Command*, pp. 20, 24. Morris sums up as follows: 'All in all the British were not thinking in imperial terms. They were rich. They were victorious.

India Company had not actually intended to govern India but to make money there,[7] which of course they did with predictable ruthlessness. But once the two sides in the British–Indian culture of politics, following the flowering of the middle-class British evangelical spirit, began to ascribe cultural meanings to the British domination, colonialism proper can be said to have begun.[8] Particularly, once the British rulers and the exposed sections of Indians internalized the colonial role definitions and began to speak, with reformist fervour, the language of the homology between sexual and political stratarchies, the battle

They were admired. They were not yet short of markets for their industries. They were strategically invulnerable, and they were preoccupied with domestic issues. When the queen was crowned, . . . we may be sure she thought little of her possessions beyond the seas. She was the island queen. . . . Even the Welsh, the Scots and the Irish were unfamiliar to her then, when the world called her kingdom simply "England". . . . No, in 1837 England seemed to need no empire, and the British people as a whole were not much interested in the colonies. How can one be expected to show an interest in a country like Canada, demanded Lord Melbourne the Prime Minister, where a salmon would not rise to a fly' (pp. 25–6, 30.)

[7] Morris, *Heaven's Command*, pp. 71–2.

[8] After the Sepoy Mutiny of 1857, however, the 'universalism' which had powered the early British reformers of Indian society had to give way to a second phase of 'tolerance' of Indian culture due to the fears of a second mutiny. But this new cultural relativism clearly drew a line between Indian culture seen as infantile and immoral and the culture of the British public school products: austere, courageous, self-controlled, 'adult men'. Lewis D. Wurgaft, 'Another Look at Prospero and Caliban: Magic and Magical Thinking in British India', mimeographed, pp. 5–6. Wurgaft bases his analysis partly on Francis Hutchins, *The Illusion of Permanence, British Imperialism in India* (Princeton: Princeton University Press, 1967). This shift to tolerance however did not change the basic relationship between the colonized. As in Albert Memmi's Africa, the 'good' and the 'bad' colonizers were but two different cogs performing equally important functions in the same machine. See Memmi's *The Colonizer and the Colonized*, translated by Howard Greenfeld (New York: Beacon, 1967); also Wurgaft, 'Another Look at Prospero and Caliban', pp. 12–13. C. Northcote Parkinson in his *East and West* (New York: Mentor, 1965), p. 216, sums it up neatly: 'It was the knowledgeable, efficient, and polite Europeans who did the serious damage.'

The whole process was part of a larger picture, which involved the rejection of Europe's pre-modern conceptualization of the East and reincorporation of the East into European consciousness according to the needs of colonialism. See Part Two below. It is interesting that for European philosophers of the eighteenth century, to men like Voltaire for example, China, perhaps, was the most advanced culture of the world. By the nineteenth century the Chinese had become, for the European literati, primitives.

for the minds of men was to a great extent won by the Raj.

Crucial to this cultural co-optation was the process psycho-analysis calls identification with the aggressor. In an oppressive situation, the process became the flip side of the theory of progress, an ontogenetic legitimacy for an ego defence often used by a normal child in an environment of childhood dependency to confront inescapable dominance by physically more powerful adults enjoying total legitimacy. In the colonial culture, identification with the aggressor bound the rulers and the ruled in an unbreakable dyadic relationship. The Raj saw Indians as crypto-barbarians who needed to further civilize themselves. It saw British rule as an agent of progress and as a mission. Many Indians in turn saw their salvation in becoming more like the British, in friendship or in enmity. They may not have fully shared the British idea of the martial races—the hyper-masculine, manifestly courageous, superbly loyal Indian castes and subcultures mirroring the British middle-class sexual stereotypes—but they did resurrect the ideology of the martial races latent in the traditional Indian concept of statecraft and gave the idea a new centrality. Many nineteenth-century Indian movements of social, religious and political reform—and many literary and art movements as well—tried to make Ksatriyahood the 'true' interface between the rulers and ruled as a new, nearly exclusive indicator of authentic Indianness. The origins and functions of this new stress on Ksatriyahood is best evidenced by the fact that, contrary to the beliefs of those carrying the psychological baggage of colonialism, the search for martial Indianness underwrote one of the most powerful collaborationist strands within the Indian society, represented by a majority of the feudal princelings in India and some of the most impotent forms of protest against colonialism (such as the immensely courageous but ineffective terrorism of Bengal, Maharashtra and Panjab led by semi-Westernized, middle-class, urban youth).

The change in consciousness that took place can be briefly stated in terms of three concepts which became central to colonial India: *purusatva* (the essence of masculinity), *nāritva* (the essence of femininity) and *klībatva* (the essence of hermaphroditism). The polarity defined by the antonymous *puruṣatva* and *nārītva* was gradually supplanted, in the colonial culture of politics, by the antonyms of *puruṣatva* and *klībatva*; femininity-in-masculinity was now perceived as the final negation of a man's political identity, a pathology more dangerous than femininity itself. Like some other cultures, including some strands of pre-modern Christianity, India too had its myths about good and bad androgynes and its ideas about valuable and despicable androgyny. Now there was an attempt to lump together all forms of androgyny and counterpoise them against undifferentiated masculinity. Rabindranath Tagore's (1861–1941) novel *Cār Adhyāy* brilliantly captures the pain which was involved in this change. The inner conflicts of the hero of the novel are modelled on the moral and political dilemmas of an actual revolutionary nationalist, who also happened to be a Catholic theologian and a Vedāntist, Brahmabandhav Upadhyay (1861–1907). Tagore's moving preface to the first edition of the novel, removed from subsequent editions because it affronted many Indians, sensed the personal tragedy of a revolutionary friend who, to fight the suffering of his people, had to move away from his own ideas of *svabhāva* and *svadharma*. It is remarkable that twenty-seven years before *Cār Adhyāy*, Tagore had dealt with the same process of cultural change in his novel *Gorā*, probably modelled on the same real-life figure and with a compatible political message.[9]

Many pre-Gandhian protest movements were co-opted by

[9] Rabindranath Tagore, 'Cār Adhyāy', *Racanāvalī* (Calcutta: West Bengal Government, 1961), pp. 875–923; 'Gorā', *Racanāvalī*, pp. 1–350. On Brahmabandhav Upadhyay see the brief article by Smaran Acharya, 'Upadhyay Brahmabandhav: Rabindra-Upanyāser Vitarkita Nāyak', *Desh*, 49(20), 20 March 1982, pp. 27–32. On Tagore's response to the criticisms of his position on extremist politics in *Cār Adhyāy*, see his 'Kaifyat' (1935), reproduced in Shuddhasatva Bosu, *Rabindranāther Cār Adhyāy* (Calcutta: Bharati Prakasani, 1979), pp. 7–10. Bosu also provides an interesting, politically relevant, analysis of the novel.

I am grateful to Ram Chandra Gandhi for pointing out to me that even Vivekananda, whose masculine Hinduism was a clear denial of the androgyny of his guru Ramakrishna Paramahamsa, himself became painfully aware of the cultural changes his Hinduism represented towards the end of his brief life. On Indian traditions of androgyny and myths about androgynes, see Wendy D. O'Flaherty, *Sexual Metaphors and Animal Symbols in Indian Mythology* (Delhi: Motilal Banarsidass,

this cultural change. They sought to redeem the Indians' masculinity by defeating the British, often fighting against hopeless odds, to free the former once and for all from the historical memory of their own humiliating defeat in violent power-play and 'tough politics'. This gave a second-order legitimacy to what in the dominant culture of the colony had already become the final differentiae of manliness: aggression, achievement, control, competition and power.[10] (I am ignoring for the moment the structural changes which gradually came to parallel this consciousness. Kenneth Ballhatchet has recently described the distant intimacy between British soldiers and administrators, on the one hand, and Indian women, on the other, which was officially promoted and in fact systematically institutionalized.[11] I am also ignoring the parallel process, reflected in the latent recognition by a number of writers,[12] that the white women in India were generally more exclusive and

---

1980) and *Women, Androgynes and Other Mythical Beasts* (Chicago: University of Chicago, 1980).

[10] This in spite of the fact that many of these characteristics were traditionally associated with femininity in India. See on this subject my 'Woman Versus Womanliness in India: An Essay in Political and Social Psychology', *Psychoanalytic Review*, 1978, 63(2), pp. 301–15. Also in *At the Edge of Psychology: Essays in Politics and Culture* (New Delhi: Oxford University Press, 1980), pp. 32–46. Thus, we find the well-meaning M. C. Mallik saying in his *Orient and Occident: A Comparative Study* (London, 1913), p. 183, quoted in Parkinson, *East and West*, p. 210: 'Europeans even of a friendly type lament the want of manliness in Indian nature and conduct. It would be strange if after so many centuries of coercion by religious, spiritual and political teachers, and of demoralizing social conditions, any manliness should survive, especially as when any sign of it is displayed by individuals, it is discouraged by parents, teachers, spiritual guides and political rulers as impertinence and disloyalty . . .' It is a minor tragedy of contemporary India that one of its finest products, Satyajit Ray, expresses the same consciousness in a more sophisticated way in his movie *Shatranj Ke Khilari*. Ray's ambivalence towards the dancing, singing poet-king who loses out to British statecraft based on *realpolitik* represents a sophisticated version of Mallik's awareness. See on this my review of the movie in 'Beyond Oriental Despotism: Politics and Femininity in Satyajit Ray', *Sunday*, Annual No., 1981, pp. 56–8.

[11] Kenneth Ballhatchet, *Race, Sex and Class Under the Raj* (London: Weidenfeld and Nicholson, 1980). I have spelt out the relationship between Ballhatchet's work and the argument of this essay in my review of it in the *Journal of Commonwealth and Comparative Politics*, 1982, 20(2), pp. 29–30.

[12] This latent recognition comes close to being manifest in E. M. Forster, who was himself a homosexual. See his *A Passage to India* (London: Arnold, 1967).

racist because they unconsciously saw themselves as the sexual competitors of Indian men, with whom their men had established an unconscious homo-eroticized bonding. It was this bonding which the 'passive resisters' and 'non-cooperators' exploited, not merely the liberal political institutions. They were helped in this by the split that had emerged in the Victorian culture between two ideals of masculinity. To draw upon Ballhatchet and others, the lower classes were expected to act out their manliness by demonstrating their sexual prowess; the upper classes were expected to affirm their masculinity through sexual distance, abstinence and self-control. The former was compatible with the style of rulership of Spanish, Portuguese and, to a lesser extent, French colonialism in Latin America and Africa; the latter was compatible with, of all things, one strand in the traditional Indian concept of manliness. The Brāhman in his cerebral, self-denying asceticism was the traditional masculine counterpoint to the more violent, 'virile', active Kṣatriya, the latter representing—however odd this may seem to the modern consciousness—the feminine principle in the cosmos. This is how traditional India imposed limits on Kṣatriyahood as a way of life. To avoid confusion, I am avoiding here the languages in which hyper-masculinity includes withdrawal from sexuality or positive androgyny.)

In such a culture, colonialism was not seen as an absolute evil. For the subjects, it was a product of one's own emasculation and defeat in legitimate power politics. For the rulers, colonial exploitation was an incidental and regrettable by-product of a philosophy of life that was in harmony with superior forms of political and economic organization. This was the consensus the rulers of India sought, consciously or unconsciously. They could not successfully rule a continent-sized polity while believing themselves to be moral cripples. They had to build bulwarks against a possible sense of guilt produced by a disjunction between their actions and what were till then, in terms of important norms of their own culture, 'true' values. On the other hand, their subjects could not collaborate on a long-term basis unless they had some acceptance of the ideology of the system, either as players or as counterplayers. This is the only way they could preserve a minimum of self-esteem in a situation of unavoidable injustice.

When such a cultural consensus grows, the main threat to the colonizers is bound to become the latent fear that the colonized will reject the consensus and, instead of trying to redeem their 'masculinity' by becoming the counterplayers of the rulers according to the established rules, will discover an alternative frame of reference within which the oppressed do not seem weak, degraded and distorted men trying to break the monopoly of the rulers on a fixed quantity of machismo. If this happens, the colonizers begin to live with the fear that the subjects might begin to see their rulers as morally and culturally inferior, and feed this information back to the rulers.[13] Colonialism minus a civilizational mission is no colonialism at all. It handicaps the colonizer much more than it handicaps the colonized.

III

I now come to the subsidiary homology between childhood and the state of being colonized which a modern colonial system

[13] I have briefly dealt with this in my 'Oppression and Human Liberation: Towards a Third World Utopia', in *The Politics of Awareness: Traditions, Tyranny and Utopias* (forthcoming); see an earlier version in *Alternatives*, 1978-9, 4(2), pp. 165-80. On this theme, see the sensitive writing of Memmi, *The Colonizer and the Colonized*. One of the best examples of the absence or erosion of civilizational mission in the colonizers is the Manchu conquest of China. The small group of conquerors became integrated in Chinese society over one or two generations and what was colonialism quickly became a variant of internal oppression. The more recent Japanese conquest of parts of China, too, failed to produce a theory of civilizational mission, though there were some efforts to do so. It is interesting that one of the main themes in these efforts was the stress on Japan's greater modernization and on her 'responsibility' to modernize other Asian societies. The modern West's contribution to Japanese society has been more wide-ranging than many believe! The British conquest of India during its first phase showed all the signs of being similarly integrated into Indian society. What probably stopped the integration was mainly the digging of the Suez Canal, which allowed the British to have stronger links with their cultural base than they previously had, and the entry into the Indian scene of British women, which, combined with the Indian caste system and the cultural self-confidence of large parts of Indian society, ensured endogamy.

almost invariably uses.[14] Colonizers, as we have known them in the last two centuries, came from complex societies with heterogeneous cultural and ethical traditions. As already noted, it is by underplaying some aspects of their culture and over-playing others that they built the legitimacy for colonialism.[15] For instance, it is impossible to build a hard, this-worldly sense of mission on the tradition to which St Francis of Assisi belonged: one perforce has to go back to St Augustine and Ignatius Loyola to do so. It is not possible to find legitimacy for the colonial theory of progress in the tradition of Johannes Eckhart, John Ruskin and Leo Tolstoy, based as it is on the rejection of the ideas of an omnipotent high technology, of hyper-competitive, achievement-oriented, over-organized private enterprise, and of aggressively proselytizing religious creeds operating on the basis of what Erik Erikson calls pseudo-species. One must find that legitimacy in utilitarians such as Jeremy Bentham and James Mill, in the socialist thinkers conceptualizing colonialism as a necessary step to progress and as a remedy for feudalism, and in those generally trying to fit the colonial experience within the mould of a doctrine of progress. (Childhood innocence serving as the prototype of primitive communism was one of Marx's main contributions to the theory of progress, which he conceptualized as a movement from prehistory to history and from infantile or low-level communism to adult communism. India to him always remained a

---

[14] My over-all theoretical understanding of this homology is in 'Reconstructing Childhood: A Critique of the Ideology of Adulthood', in *The Politics of Awareness: Traditions, Tyranny and Utopias* (forthcoming). A briefer version in *Resurgence*, May 1982, and in *The Times of India*, 2, 3 and 4 February 1982. In the context of India, see a discussion of such a relationship in Bruce Mazlish, *James and John Mill: Father and Son in the Nineteenth Century* (New York: Basic Books, 1975), particularly Chapter 6, pp. 116–45. For a brief introduction to the over-all picture of the assimilation of new worlds by the West (which set the context for the homology among childhood, primitivism and colonial subjugation to emerge) see Michael T. Ryan, 'Assimilating New Worlds in the Sixteenth and Seventeenth Centuries', *Comparative Studies in Society and History*, 1981, 23(4), pp. 519–38. Ryan mentions 'the tendency to compare—if not confuse—ancients with exotics', as also its relationship with the existing body of demonological theory in Europe.

[15] Memmi, in *The Colonizer and the Colonized*, has graphically described the process through which the new entrant is broken into the ruling culture of the colonizer.

country of 'small semi-barbarian, semi-civilized communities', which 'restricted the human mind within the smallest possible compass, making it the unresisting tool of superstition' and where the peasants lived their 'undignified, stagnant and vegetative life'. 'These little communities', Marx argued, '. . . brought about a brutalising worship of nature exhibiting its degradation in the fact that man, the sovereign of nature, fell down on his knees in the adoration of *Kanuman* [sic], monkey. and *Sabbala*, the cow.' It followed, according to Marx, that 'whatever may have been the crime of England she was the unconscious tool of history'.[16] Such a view was bound to contribute handsomely—even if inadvertently—to the racist world view and ethnocentrism that underlay colonialism.[17] A similar, though less influential, cultural role was played by some of Freud's early disciples who went out to 'primitive' societies to pursue the homology between primitivism and infantility.[18] They, too, were working out the cultural and psychological implications of the biological principle 'ontogeny recapitulates phylogeny', and that of the ideology of 'normal', fully socialized, male adulthood. Only, unlike the utilitarians and the Marxists, they did not clearly identify primitivism and infantility with disvalues like structural simplicity and 'static history'.[19])

There was blood-curdling shadow-boxing among the com-

[16] Karl Marx, 'The British Rule in India' (1853), in Karl Marx and F. Engels, *Articles on Britain* (Moscow: Progress Publishers, 1971), pp. 166–72; see especially pp. 171–2.

[17] These imageries provided the psychological basis of the theory of the Asiatic mode of production. I am grateful to Giri Deshingkar for pointing out to me that the Communist Party of China tried to escape this Marxian double-bind by passing an official resolution in 1927 that China was not an Asiatic society. Such are the pulls of scientific social sciences.

[18] That another view of primitivism is possible, more or less within the same framework, is shown by the political use of Freud's concept of the polymorphous perverse infant in a contemporary Marxist, Herbert Marcuse, in *Eros and Civilization* (London: Sphere, 1969). Before him Wilhelm Reich in psychoanalysis, D. H. Lawrence in literature and Salvador Dali in art had explored the creative possibilities of primitivism within a meta-Freudian framework.

[19] See on this theme O. Mannoni, 'Psychoanalysis and the Decolonization of Mankind', in J. Miller (ed.), *Freud* (London: Weidenfeld and Nicholson, 1972), pp. 86–95.

peting Western schools of social philosophy, including the various versions of Western Christianity. But there can be no doubt about which sub-tradition in Europe was the stronger. There was an almost complete consensus among the sensitive European intellectuals that colonialism was an evil, albeit a necessary one. It was the age of optimism in Europe. Not only the arch-conservatives and the apologists of colonialism were convinced that one day their cultural mission would be complete and the barbarians would become civilized; even the radical critics of Western society were convinced that colonialism was a necessary stage of maturation for some societies. They differed from the imperialists, only in that they did not expect the colonized to love, or be grateful to the colonizers for introducing their subjects to the modern world.[20] Thus, in the eyes of the European civilization the colonizers were not a group of self-seeking, rapacious, ethnocentric vandals and self-chosen carriers of a cultural pathology, but ill-intentioned, flawed instruments of history, who unconsciously worked for the upliftment of the underprivileged of the world.

The growth of this ideology paralleled a major cultural reconstruction that took place in the West during the first phase of colonialism, the phase in which colonialism was becoming consolidated as an important cultural process and a way of life for the Spanish and the Portuguese. Philippe Aries argues that the modern concept of childhood is a product of seventeenth-century Europe.[21] Before then the child was seen as a smaller version of the adult; now the child became—this Aries does not fully recognize—an inferior version of the adult and had to be educated through the newly-expanded period of childhood.

---

[20] On the sense of betrayal which British colonialists had because of the 'ungratefulness' of Indians, seen as a cultural feature, see Wurgaft, 'Another Look at Prospero and Caliban'. Wurgaft obviously borrows from O. Mannoni, *Prospero and Caliban: The Psychology of Colonization*, trans. Pamela Powes (New York: Frederick A. Praeger, 1964), 2nd edition.

[21] Philippe Aries, *Centuries of Childhood: A Social History of Family Life*, trans. Robert Baldick (New York: Knopf, 1962). For a different point of view, see Lloyd deMause 'The Evolution of Childhood', in deMause (ed.), *The History of Childhood* (New York: The Psychohistory Press, 1974), pp. 1-73.

(A parallel and contemporary development in Europe was the emergence of the modern concept of womanhood, underwritten by the changing concept of Christian godhead which, under the influence of Protestantism, became more masculine.[22])

The new concept of childhood bore a direct relationship to the doctrine of progress now regnant in the West. Childhood now no longer seemed only a happy, blissful prototype of beatific angels, as it had in the peasant cultures of Europe only a century earlier. It increasingly looked like a blank slate on which adults must write their moral codes—an inferior version of maturity, less productive and ethical, and badly contaminated by the playful, irresponsible and spontaneous aspects of human nature. Concurrently, probably propelled by what many Weberians have identified as the prime mover behind the modernization of West Europe, the Protestant Ethic, it became the responsibility of the adult to 'save' the child from a state of unrepentant, reprobate sinfulness through proper socialization, and help the child grow towards a Calvinist ideal of adulthood and maturity. Exploitation of children in the name of putting them to productive work, which took place in the early days of the Industrial Revolution in Britain, was a natural corollary of such a concept of childhood.[23]

Colonialism dutifully picked up these ideas of growth and development and drew a new parallel between primitivism and childhood. Thus, the theory of social progress was telescoped not merely into the individual's life-cycle in Europe but also into the area of cultural differences in the colonies.[24] What was childlikeness of the child and childishness of immature adults now also became the lovable and unlovable savagery of primi-

[22] Nandy, 'Woman Versus Womanliness'.

[23] See Nandy, 'Reconstructing Childhood'.

[24] V. G. Kiernan says in the context of Africa in his *The Lords of Human Kind: European Attitudes to the Outside World in the Imperial Age* (Harmondsworth: Penguin, 1972), p. 243: 'The notion of the African as a minor, endorsed at times even by a Livingstone, took very strong hold. Spaniards and Boers had questioned whether natives had souls: modern Europeans cared less about that but doubted whether they had minds, or minds capable of adult growth. A theory came to be fashionable that mental growth in the African ceased early, that childhood was never left behind.'

tives and the primitivism of subject societies. This version of
the theory of progress is summarized below.

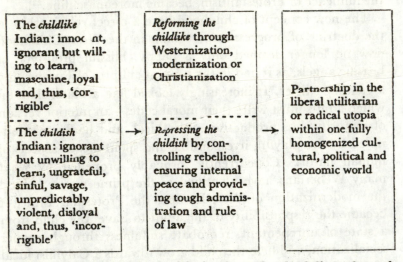

The *childlike* Indian: innocent, ignorant but willing to learn, masculine, loyal and, thus, 'corrigible'	Reforming the *childlike* through Westernization, modernization or Christianization	
The *childish* Indian: ignorant but unwilling to learn, ungrateful, sinful, savage, unpredictably violent, disloyal and, thus, 'incorrigible' →	Repressing the *childish* by controlling rebellion, ensuring internal peace and providing tough administration and rule of law →	Partnership in the liberal utilitarian or radical utopia within one fully homogenized cultural, political and economic world

One element in the legitimization of colonialism through
reconstruing the human life cycle has not been touched upon.
Not that it was unimportant in the colonial culture; but it was,
I suspect, specific to India and China and, to that extent, less
generally applicable to modern colonialism. I shall briefly say
something about it now.

Modern Europe had delegitimized not merely femininity and
childhood but also old age.[25] Judaeo-Christianity always had
an element which saw aging as a natural unfolding and result
of man's essential sinfulness. The decomposition of the human
body was seen as only an indicator of the evil in the one degenerating: according to the old South European saying, till
youth a person looked the way god made him; after that he
looked the way he really was. With increasing stress on the
reprobate nature of man, it was this postulate which came to
the fore in Europe's new ideology of male adulthood, completing the picture of a world where only the adult male
reflected a reasonable approximation of a perfect human being.

[25] See a brief statement of the problem in its interrelatedness with colonial encounters in my 'The Politics of Life Cycle', *Mazingira* (forthcoming).

The elderly (representing wisdom and the negation of 'pure' intellect) were now increasingly seen as socially irrelevant because of their low physical power and because their social productivity and cultural role could not be easily quantified. I need hardly add that, given the nature of available technology, the ideological changes neatly fitted the emerging principles of 'productive' work and 'performance' as they were monetized and enshrined in new political and social institutions.

This part of the ideology of male-adulthood too was exported to the colonies in a few chosen cases. Kiernan does refer to the ideological problem of British colonialism in India which could not easily grapple with the fact that India had a civilization, howsoever strange by European standards. Newly-discovered Africa, with its strong emphasis on the folk, the oral and the rural could be more easily written off as savage. It was more difficult to do so for India and China which the European Orientalists and even the first generation rulers had studied and, sometimes, venerated. And, everything said, there were the traditions of four thousand years of civic living, a well-developed *literati* tradition (in spite of all its stress on oral cultures), and alternative traditions of philosophy, art and science which often attracted the best minds of Europe. The fact that India's past was living (unlike, say, pre-Islamic Egypt) complicated the situation. Some explanation had to be given for her political and cultural 'degradation'.

The colonial ideology handled the problem in two mutually inconsistent ways. Firstly, it postulated a clear disjunction between India's past and its present. The civilized India was in the bygone past; now it was dead and 'museumized'. The present India, the argument went, was only nominally related to its history; it was India only to the extent it was a senile, decrepit version of her once-youthful, creative self. As a popular myth would have it, Max Müller, for all his pioneering work in Indology and love for India, forbade his students to visit India; to him, the India that was living was not the true India and the India that was true had to be but dead.

Secondly and paradoxically, the colonial culture postulated

that India's later degradation was not due to colonial rule —which, if anything, had improved Indian culture by fighting against its irrational, oppressive, retrogressive elements —but due to aspects of the traditional Indian culture which in spite of some good points carried the seeds of India's later cultural downfall. Like a sinful man Indian culture was living through a particularly debilitating senility. (The very fact that Hinduism did not have in its concept of *pāpa* the strong inner-directed connotations of the Christian, post-reformation concept of sin was itself seen as one of the main proofs of India's fatal cultural flaw. Even a man like Albert Schweitzer did not remain uncontaminated by this ideology; he made it a central plank of his interpretation of Hinduism.[26]) Thus, in this argument, there was a postulate of continuity but it applied more to sinfulness than to virtues; for an explanation of India's virtues one had to fall back upon her contacts with the modern world.

IV

What were the main dimensions of the efforts to reorder Indian culture in response to and as a part of these colonial categories? The answer is best given in terms of a few of the nineteenth-century figures who revalued the traditional Hindu orientations to the male and the female, and coped with the modern concepts of mature, adult normality as opposed to abnormal, immature, infantile primitivism.[27]

Probably the person who most dramatically sought to redefine popular mythology to fit the changing values under colonialism was Michael Madhusudan Dutt (1824–73) whose Bengali epic *Meghnādvadh Kāvya* was hailed, in his lifetime, as one of the greatest literary efforts of all time in Bengali.[28]

[26] Albert Schweitzer, *Hindu Thought and Its Development* (New York: Beacon, 1959).

[27] The examples I shall use will be mainly from Bengal, not merely because the Bengali culture best illustrated—and dramatized—the colonial predicament in India's political, cultural and creative life, but also because it was in Bengal that the Western intrusion was the deepest and the colonial presence the longest.

[28] 'Meghnādvadh Kāvya', 1861, Kshetra Gupta (ed.), *Madhusudan Racanāvali*, vols. 1 and 2 (Calcutta: Sahitya Samsad, 1965), pp. 35–117.

Madhusudan, flamboyantly Westernized in life style and ideology—he had even embraced the Church of England's version of Christianity and declared that he cared only 'a pin's head for Hinduism'—first wanted to make his mark in English literature. But he returned to his mother tongue within a decade to write brilliant interpretations of some of the Purāṇic epics. *Meghnādvadh* was the greatest of them all.

As is well known, *Meghnādvadh* retells the Rāmāyaṇa, turning the traditionally sacred figures of Rāma and Lakṣmaṇa into weak-kneed, passive-aggressive, feminine villains and the demons Rāvaṇa and his son Meghnād into majestic, masculine, modern heroes. It interprets the encounter between Rāma and Rāvaṇa as a political battle, with morality on the side of the demons. The epic ends with the venal gods defeating and killing the courageous, proud, achievement-oriented, competitive, efficient, technologically superior, 'sporting' demons symbolized by Meghnād.

Meghnādvadh was not the first reinterpretation of the Rāmāyaṇa. In south India, an alternative tradition of Rāmāyaṇa, which antedated Madhusudan, had off and on been a source of social conflict and controversy. In Jainism, too, a version of the Rāmāyaṇa had been sometimes a source of intercommunal conflicts.[29] In any case, Rāma, however godlike, was traditionally not the final repository of all good. Unlike the Semitic gods, he was more human and more overtly a mix of the good and the bad, the courageous and the cowardly, the male and the female. Rāvaṇa, too, had never been traditionally all bad. He was seen as having a record of genuine spiritual achievements.

Madhusudan Dutt therefore was in the living tradition of dissent in India. (This dissent did not become a political absurdity because he lived towards the end of the period during which the British, though politically the most powerful, were still only one of many forces in India and the Western culture

[29] At least one literary critic, it seems, has traced the source of Madhusudan's reinterpretation of Rāmāyaṇa to his probable exposure to the Jain Rāmāyaṇa while he was in Madras. Asit Bandopadhyay, *Ādhunik Bāṅglā Sāhityer Saṃkṣipta Itivṛtta*, 1965, cited in Bishwanath Bandopadhyay, 'Pramilār Utsa', *Desh*, 49(18), 6 March 1982.

was a manageable vector within India; Westernism enjoyed the support of only small minorities of both the rulers and the ruled.) Simultaneously, Madhusudan's criterion for reversing the roles of Rāma and Rāvaṇa, as expressed in their characters, was a direct response to the colonial situation. He admired Rāvaṇa for his masculine vigour, accomplished warriorhood, and his sense of *realpolitik* and history; he accepted Rāvaṇa's 'adult' and 'normal' commitments to secular, possessive this-worldliness and his consumer's lust for life. On the other hand, he despised 'Rāma and his rabble'—the expression was his—because they were effeminate, ineffective pseudo-ascetics, who were austere not by choice but because they were weak.

There was an obvious political meaning in the contradiction Madhusudan posed in a culture which rejected most forms of competitive individual achievement, frequently underplayed sex-role differences, gave low status to high technology, granted equal status to myth and history, and rejected hedonism, including possessive individualism and consumerism. This is not to say that the values Rāvaṇa articulated were alien to the Indian traditions: in fact, they were sometimes associated with mythical figures who evoked admiration and respect. But on the whole they had been contained or marginalized as so many culturally-defined esoterica. Rāvaṇa himself, after all, was seen as someone who knew the Vedas well and had won his powers from sacred sources through years of *tapas*. His good qualities, however, were recognized within the constraints of his *rākṣasa* self. Madhusudan now freed Rāvaṇa from these traditional constraints to give him a new stature as a scientific, learned, modern Kṣatriya king, fighting the non-secular politics and anti-technologism of a banished pastoral prince.

Meghnādvadh was a tragedy. Madhusudan's heroes were, to a point, oddities in a culture which apparently had no tradition of tragedy. However, to get the full meaning of this deviation, one must recognize that in the Purāṇic tradition there *was* a distinctive concept of the tragic in life and letters. Tragedy in the Purāṇas did not centre around a grand final defeat or death of the hero, or around the final victory of the ungodly. Tragedy lay in the majestic sweep of time and in the unavoidable decline or decay that informed the mightiest and the humblest, the epochal and the trivial, and the 'permanent' and the transient. In the Mahābhārata, the self-chosen and yet fated *mahāprasthāna* or the great departure of the Pāṇḍavas after their climactic victory in the battle at Kurukṣetra and the death of god Kṛṣṇa —lonely, aged, nostalgic, and partly forgotten—are good examples of what I am trying to convey.

Meghnādvadh represented a different concept of tragedy. Not only were the good and the evil clearly separated in the epic, according to well-defined ethical criteria, but evil finally triumphed. Traditionally the *rākṣasas* represented a demonic version of masculinity which was unfettered by dominant norms and traditions. Now aspects of this demonic masculinity were endorsed, for the Indians, by the new culture of colonialism and the variation on the myth of the Promethean man it popularized. By making *Meghnādvadh* a tragedy, by inducing his readers to identify with his heroes, Madhusudan legitimized the personality type portrayed by his heroes and underwrote the emerging ideology of modernity as well as compatible concepts of masculinity and adulthood in his community's world view. What was recessive and in fetters in traditional Indian masculinity was now made salient with the help of existing cultural imagery and myths.

This is how Madhusudan updated the early cultural criticisms of Rammohun Roy (1772–1833).[30] Rammohun had introduced into the culture of India's expanding urban middle classes—for the sake of those alienated from the older life style and values by the colonial intrusion into eastern India—the ideas of organized religion, a sacred text, monotheism and, above all, a patriarchal godhead. Simultaneously he had 'misread' the nondualism of Śankarācārya to suggest a new definition of masculinity, based on the demystification of womanhood

[30] See Nandy, 'Sati: A Nineteenth Century Tale of Women, Violence and Protest', in *At the Edge of Psychology*, pp. 1–31, for a discussion of the psychological dimensions of Rammohun Roy's response to colonialism. The paper also discusses the personal and cultural ambivalence which powered Rammohun Roy's philosophy of social change.

and on the shifting of the locus of magicality from everyday
femininity to a transcendent male principle. He had sought to
liberate woman from the responsibility she bore in the shared
consciousness—or unconsciousness—for failures of nurture in
nature, politics and social life. Madhusudan, on the other hand,
innocent of the questions Rammohun had raised in his philosophy of reform, tried to contain within the Indian world view
Western concepts of the male and the female, and the adult
and the infantile, and thus to make the Western presence in
India seem natural in a context where the West had seemingly
come to represent, for many Indians, the more valued aspects
of Indian culture. The previously rejected hyper-masculine
rākṣasa qualities of Rāvaṇa became now the heroic qualities of
a demon-king representing true, adult masculinity; and the
many-faceted, open personality of Rāma, on whom successive
generations of Indians had projected their complex concepts of
goodness, became a non-masculine, immature, effete godhead,
representing a lower—perhaps even false—concept of goodness.

This is not the place to discuss the Oedipal passions which
pushed Madhusudan towards a new definition of masculinity
and normality. The point to remember is that his efforts, on
behalf of his culture, to 'tame' the Western concepts of manhood and womanhood were made when the full power and
glory of British imperialism were not yet apparent. As a result,
there was little defensiveness in him. His aggressive criticism
of Indian traditions was in the style of the major reform movements of India: it was not merely an attempt to explain Indian
culture in Indian terms, or even in Western terms, but was an
attempt to explain the West in Indian terms and to incorporate
it in the Indian culture as an unavoidable experience.

I now turn to the second stream of cultural criticism in response
to colonialism, once again grounded in reinterpreted sacred
texts but in reality dependent on core values borrowed from
the colonial world view and then legitimized according to
existing concepts of sacredness. Probably the most creative
representative of this stream was Bankimchandra Chatterjee

(1838–94) whose novels and essays were an attempt to marginalize the earlier model of critical Hinduism and suggest a new framework of political culture which projected into the Hindu past, into a lost golden age of Hinduism, the qualities of Christianity which seemingly gave Christians their strength.

Ānandamath, a novel which became the Bible of the first generation of Indian nationalists, particularly the Bengali terrorists, was a direct attempt to work out the implications of such a concept of religion.[31] The order of the *sannyāsis* in the novel was obviously the Hindu counterpart of the priesthood in some versions of Western Christianity. In fact, their Westernness gave them their sense of history, their stress on an organized religion, and above all, their acceptance of the Raj as a transient but historically inevitable and legitimate phenomenon in Hindu terms.

But it was Bankimchandra's elegant essay on Kṛṣṇa which provided the missing link—a reinterpreted traditional godhead —to the new model of Hinduism.[32] What Madhusudan sought to do in the context of the Rāmāyaṇa, Bankimchandra sought to do in the context of the Mahābhārata and the five Purāṇas dealing with Kṛṣṇa. He tried to build a historical and a historically conscious Kṛṣṇa—self-consistent, self-conscious and moral according to modern norms. He scanned all the ancient texts of Kṛṣṇa, not only to locate Kṛṣṇa in history, but to argue away all references to Kṛṣṇa's character traits unacceptable to the new norms relating to sexuality, politics and social relationships. His Kṛṣṇa was not the soft, childlike, self-contradictory, sometimes immoral being—a god who could blend with the everyday life of his humble devotees and who was only occasionally a successful, activist, productive and chastising god operating in the company of the great. Bankimchandra did not adore Kṛṣṇa as a child-god or as a playful—sometimes sexually playful—adolescent who was simultaneously an androgynous,

---

[31] Bankimchandra Chatterji, *Racanāvalī*, with an introduction by Jogesh Bagal (Calcutta: Sahitya Samsad, 1958), vol. 1, pp. 715–88.

[32] Bankimchandra Chatterji, 'Kṛṣṇacaritra', 1886, in *Racanāvalī*, vol. 2, pp. 407–583.

philosophically sensitive, practical idealist. His Kṛṣṇa was a respectable, righteous, didactic, 'hard' god, protecting the glories of Hinduism as a proper religion and preserving it as an internally consistent moral and cultural system. Bankim-chandra rejected as latter-day interpolations—and hence un-authentic—every trait of Kṛṣṇa that did not meet the first requirement for a Christian and Islamic god, namely all-perfection.[33] His goal was to make Kṛṣṇa a normal, non-pagan male god who would not humiliate his devotees in front of the progressive Westerners.

It was this consciousness which Swami Dayanand Saraswati (1824–83) and Swami Vivekananda (1863–1902) shared and developed further. The two Swamis entered the scene when the colonial culture had made deeper inroads into Indian society. It was no longer possible to give priority to cultural reform over mass politics without ignoring the fact that a psychological invasion from the West had begun with the widespread internalization of Western values by many Indians, and an over-emphasis on the reform of the Indian personality could only open up new, invidious modes of Westernization.

Yet, this is exactly what the two redoubtable Swamis did. They borrowed their fundamental values from the Western world view and, in spite of their image as orthodox revivalists, were ruthlessly critical of the Hindus. They also took the position that the Hindus had been great—which meant, in their terms, virile and adult—in ancient times and had fallen on bad days because of their loss of contact with textual Brahminism and true Kṣatriyahood. Obviously, if *kṣātratej* or martial valour was the first differentia of a ruler, the ruler who had greater *kṣātratej* deserved to rule. This was hardly a compliment to the living Hindus; if anything, it perfectly fitted the dominant structure of colonial thought,[34] as well as the ideology of some Western Orientalists.

Thus, Vivekananda and Dayanand, too, tried to Christianize

[33] This itself was modern. In an ahistorical or epic culture, temporality cannot be allowed to determine authenticity. See Section VII of the essay.

[34] Kiernan, *The Lords of Human Kind.*

Hinduism, particularly the dominant Hindu concept of the desirable person. In doing so, they identified the West with power and hegemony, which in turn they identified with a superior civilization. Then they tried to 'list' the differences between the West and India and attributed the former's superiority to these differences. The rest of their lives they spent exhorting the hapless Hindus to pursue these cultural differentiae of the West. And predictably they found out—Indian culture being the complex, open-ended system it is—that traditions supporting some of the valued Western traits were there in Hinduism but were lost on the 'unworthy' contemporary Hindus. Predictably, too, the main elements of their Hinduism were, again: an attempt to turn Hinduism into an organized religion with an organized priesthood, church and missionaries; acceptance of the idea of proselytization and religious 'conscientization' (*śuddhi*, the *bête noire* of the Indian Christians and Muslims, was a Semitic element introduced into nineteenth-century Hinduism under the influences of Western Christianity); an attempt to introduce the concept of The Book following the Semitic creeds (the Vedas and the Gītā in the case of the two Swamis); the acceptance of the idea of linear, objective and causal history; acceptance of ideas akin to monotheism (Vivekananda even managed to produce that rare variant of it: a quasi-monotheistic creed with a feminine godhead as its central plank); and a certain puritanism and this-worldly asceticism borrowed partly from the Catholic church and partly from Calvinism.

Such a model was bound to lead to the perception that the loss of masculinity and cultural regression of the Hindus was due to the loss of the original Aryan qualities which they shared with the Westerners. There *was* a political meaning in Dayanand's decision to call his church Arya Samaj. It was also bound to lead to an emphasis on basic psychological and institutional changes in Hinduism and to the rejection of other forms of critical Hinduism, which stressed the primacy of political changes and sought to give battle to British colonialism by accepting the contemporary Hindus *as they were*. (For instance,

Gandhi later on organized the Hindus as Indians, not as Hindus, and granted Hinduism the right to maintain its character as an unorganized, anarchic, open-ended faith.) Not surprisingly, the second model gradually became incompatible with the needs of anti-colonialism and, by over-stressing exogenous categories of self-criticism, indirectly collaborationist.

There was yet another political paradox in which the model was caught. While in the first phase of the Raj the rulers supported political participation of the Hindus (because such participation by the then pro-British Hindus was advantageous to the regime), in the second phase, the rulers discouraged it because of growing nationalism. Similarly, while in the first phase the regime frowned upon all social reform movements and often took decades to pass laws on any Indian social practice against which Indian reformers fought, in the second phase they promoted those schools of nationalism which expected political freedom to follow from social reform, particularly the reform of Indian national character.

Though there were instances of deviation even among those who accepted the second model of critical Hinduism, such as the great bravery and immense sacrifices made for the nationalist cause by the terrorists and by their larger-than-life versions like Vinayak D. Savarkar and Subhas Chandra Bose, the model *did* allow Western cultural ideas to percolate to the deepest levels of Hindu religious ideas and accepted Western cultural theories of political subjugation and economic backwardness. The newly created sense of linear history in Hinduism—an internalized counterpart of the Western theory of progress—was a perfect instrument for this purpose. It allowed one to project into history the sense of inferiority *vis-à-vis* an imperial faith and to see the golden age of Hinduism as an ancient version of the modern West.[35]

In short, both streams of political consciousness, though seemingly hostile to each other, produced partly-colonial designs of

[35] In fact, the anti-Muslim stance of much of Hindu nationalism can be construed as partly a displaced hostility against the colonial power which could not be

cultural and political selfhood for the colonized. Actually the first, evolved by the likes of Rammohun Roy, was based, experientially at least, on greater self-esteem and autonomy, though later on it was to seem—as well as to become—more subservient to the Western world view, both to its opponents and its supporters.

It only slowly became obvious to those living with the full-grown culture of British colonialism that neither of the two models could provide an adequate basis for self-esteem and cultural autonomy. Yet, there was no alternative model in sight that could take a critical look at Indian traditions, evaluate the nature of the Western impact on them, and update Indian culture without disturbing its authenticity.

However, some scattered efforts were made to break out of this stagnation in the nineteenth century itself. Persons like Iswarchandra Vidyasagar (1820–91) *did* seek to create a new political awareness which would combine a critical awareness of Hinduism and colonialism with cultural and individual authenticity. It is thus that they emerged, as a biographer seems to recognize in the case of Vidyasagar, 'whole and enriched from the clash of cultures . . . in the nineteenth century'.[36] Iswarchandra too fought institutionalized violence against Indian women, giving primacy to social reform over politics. But his diagnosis of Hinduism did not grow out of feelings of cultural inferiority; it grew out of perceived contradictions within Hinduism itself. Even when he fought for Indian women, he did not operate on the basis of Westernized ideals of masculinity and femininity or on the basis of a theory of cultural progress. He refused to Semiticize Hinduism and adopt the result as a ready-made theory of state. As a result, his society could neither ignore nor forgive him. (The pandit, when he was

---

expressed directly because of the new legitimacy created within Hinduism for this power. Such a dynamic would seem to roughly duplicate the displacement of Oedipal hostilities in the authoritarian personality. Cf. T. W. Adorno, Else Frenkel-Brunswik, D. Levinson and R. N. Sanford, *The Authoritarian Personality* (New York: Harper, 1960).

[36] Amalesh Tripathi, *Vidyasagar: The Traditional Modernizer* (Calcutta: Orient Longman, 1974).

dying, could hear the bands playing outside his house, celebrating his approaching death.) Vidyasagar's Hinduism looked dangerously like Hinduism and hence subversive to the orthodox Hindus. Simultaneously, his cultural criticisms seemed fundamental even to those allegiant to the other two models of internal criticism and cultural change. He could be ignored neither as an apostate nor as an apologist.

Vidyasagar acquired this cultural embedding by eschewing some of the normative and institutional goals of the competing models. He refused to use the imagery of a golden age of the Hindus from which contemporary Hindus had allegedly fallen, he refused to be psychologically tied to the history of non-Hindu rule of India, he resisted reading Hinduism as a 'proper religion' in the Islamic or Western sense, he rejected the ideologies of masculinity and adulthood, and he refused to settle scores with the West by creating a nation of super-Hindus or by defending Hinduism as an all-perfect antidote to Western cultural encroachment. His was an effort to protect not the formal structure of Hinduism but its spirit, as an open, anarchic federation of sub-cultures and textual authorities which allowed new readings and internal criticisms.

Thus, Iswarchandra's anti-colonialism was not defined by the Western version of rationalism, the popular Bengali *bhadralok* stereotypes about him notwithstanding. It was also not heavily reactive, though that impression too was created by some elements of his everyday life (including his aggressively Indian dress, interpersonal style and food habits).[37] He was first and foremost a Brāhmaṇ pandit, a man of learning and a polemicist with a clear position on sacred texts which he saw as congruent with his reforms.[38] He was not even a man of religion out to sell a new version of Hinduism and, unlike Gandhi, he did not face the imposition of any mahatmahood on

[37] Benoy Ghose, *Vidyāsāgar o Bāṅgāli Samāj*, vols. 1–3 (Calcutta: Bengal Publishers, 1973), 2nd ed; Indra Mitra, *Karuṇāsāgar Vidyāsāgar* (Calcutta: Ananda Publishers, 1971).

[38] Tripathi, *Vidyasagar*, Chapter 1. The problems involved in this reinterpretive mode have been touched upon by Asok Sen, *Iswarchandra Vidyasagar and His Elusive Milestones* (Calcutta: Riddhi India, 1977).

him. But, like Gandhi, he could have declared himself an orthodox Hindu and claimed his Hinduism better than that of his opponents because it encompassed the colonial experience.

Though Iswarchandra came from a poor rural background, his times did not allow him to take his dissent outside the urban middle classes, to mobilize the peripheries of his society, or to make a more creative use of folk—as opposed to Sanskritic—Hinduism. But his model did resolutely resist the ideology of hyper-masculinity and 'normality'. Popular readings of Iswarchandra recognized this. Madhusudan Dutt once wrote that the obstinate fiery Brāhman had 'a Bengali mother's heart' and during Vidyasagar's own lifetime the Sanskrit saying 'tougher than thunder and softer than flower' became a standard, if trite, account of his androgyny. There was an implicit awareness all around that his combination of aggressive defiance of authority and authoritative reinterpretations of authority challenged some of the basic postulates of the colonial theory of progress, particularly the joint construction of 'legitimate inequality' by the Indians and the British. If Iswarchandra failed to fully politicize this dissent, he at least sought to make instrumental use of the transient, 'unavoidable' oppression of colonialism to meet India's needs. And this, without accepting the Western utilitarian, social Darwinist, and radical conceptions of these needs.

V

The problem of colonization did not only concern the overseas countries. The process of decolonization—which is in any case far from complete in those countries—is also under way at home, in our schools, in female demands for equality, in the education of small children and in many other fields. . . . If certain cultures prove capable of destroying others . . . the destructive forces brought forth by these cultures also act internally. . . .

O. Mannoni[39]

The colonizer, who in order to ease his conscience gets into the habit of seeing the other man as *an animal*, accustoms himself to treating him like an animal, and tends objectively to transform

[39] Mannoni, 'Psychoanalysis', pp. 93-4.

himself into an animal. . . . They thought they were only slaugh-
tering Indians, or Hindus, or South Sea Islanders, or Africans.
They have in fact overthrown, one after another, the ramparts
behind which European civilization could have developed
freely.

Aimé Césaire[40]

The broad psychological contours of colonialism are now
known. Thanks to sensitive writers like Octave Mannoni,
Frantz Fanon and Albert Memmi we even know something
about the interpersonal patterns which constituted the colonial
situation, particularly in Africa.[41] Less well-known are the
cultural and psychological pathologies produced by colonization in the colonizing societies.

As folk wisdom would have it, the only sufferers of colonialism are the subject communities. Colonialism, according to this
view, is the name of a political economy which ensures a one-
way flow of benefits, the subjects being the perpetual losers in
a zero-sum game and the rulers the beneficiaries. This is a
view of human mind and history promoted by colonialism itself. This view has a vested interest in denying that the colonizers are at least as much affected by the ideology of colonialism, that their degradation, too, can sometimes be terrifying.
Behind all the rhetoric of the European intelligentsia on the
evils of colonialism lay their unstated faith that the gains from
colonialism to Europe, to the extent that they primarily involved material products, were real, and the losses, to the
extent they involved social relations and psychological states,
false. To venture a less popular interpretation of colonialism—
which I hope is relatively less contaminated by the ideology of
colonialism—I shall produce examples from the experience of
one of the world's stablest and most subtly-managed colonial
polities of all times, British India. These examples will show
that what Aimé Césaire calls the 'decivilization' of the colonizers is not an impotent fantasy after all, that it is an empirical

[40] Aimé Césaire, *Discourse on Colonialism*, trans. Joan Pinkham (New York and
London: Monthly Review Press, 1972), pp. 20, 57–8.
[41] Mannoni, *Prospero and Caliban*; Fanon, *Black Skin, White Masks*; Memmi, *The
Colonizer and the Colonized*.

reality of the kind on which even Mannoni and Fanon can agree.[42] Fanon describes a police officer who, as he tortured the freedom fighters in Algeria, became violent towards his own wife and children.[43] Even from Fanon's impassioned political psychiatry, it becomes obvious that the officer *had* to do within his family—and within himself—what he did to the freedom fighters. Colonialism as a psychological process cannot but endorse the principle of isomorphic oppressions which restates for the era of the psychological man the ancient wisdom implied in the New Testament and also perhaps in the Sauptik Parva of the Mahābhārata: 'Do not do unto others what you would that they do not do unto you, lest you do unto yourself what you do unto others.'

The impact of colonialism on India was deep. The economic exploitation, psychological uprooting and cultural disruption it caused were tremendous.[44] But India was a country of hundreds of millions living in a large land mass. In spite of the presence of a paramount power which acted as the central authority, the country was culturally fragmented and politically heterogeneous. It could, thus, partly confine the cultural impact of imperialism to its urban centres, to its Westernized

[42] Césaire, *Discourse on Colonialism*, p. 13. The psychological principle involved was recognized by Plato himself. As Iris Murdoch sums up in her *The Fire and the Sun: Why Plato Banished the Artists* (Oxford: Oxford University Press, 1977), p. 39: 'Whatever his [Plato's] dogma, there is little doubt about his psychology.... We cannot escape the causality of sin. We are told in the *Theaetetus* (176–7) that the inescapable penalty of wickedness is simply to be the sort of person one is.' It is surprising that Fanon, whom Peter Berger calls the 'Clausewitz of Revolution' had only limited awareness of the creative possibilities of such a philosophy of evil.

[43] Frantz Fanon, *The Wretched of the Earth* (Harmondsworth: Penguin, 1967), pp. 215–17.

[44] The political and economic dislocation is of course well known and well documented. For an early discussion of the economic exploitation under British colonialism, see for example R. C. Dutt, *Economic History of India in the Victorian Age* (London: Routledge and Kegan Paul, 1903) and Dadabhoi Naoroji, *Poverty and Un-British Rule in India* (1901), (New Delhi: Publications Division, 1969). For instances of cultural and psychological pathology produced by colonization in India, see R. C. Majumdar, A. K. Majumdar and D. K. Ghose (eds.), *British Paramountcy and Indian Renaissance*, part 2 (Bombay: Bharatiya Vidya Bhavan, 1965). For a case study of a specific cultural pathology under the Raj, see for instance, my 'Sati'.

and semi-Westernized upper and middle classes, and to some
sections of its traditional élites. That was not the case for the
rulers from a relatively more homogeneous small island. They
were overwhelmed by the experience of being colonial rulers.
As a result, the long-term cultural damage colonialism did to
the British society was greater.

Firstly, the experience of colonizing did not leave the internal
culture of Britain untouched. It began to bring into prominence
those parts of the British political culture which were least
tender and humane. It de-emphasized speculation, intellection
and *caritas* as feminine, and justified a limited cultural role for
women—and femininity—by holding that the softer side of
human nature was irrelevant to the public sphere. It openly
sanctified—in the name of such values as competition, achievement, control and productivity—new forms of institutionalized
violence and ruthless social Darwinism.[45] The instrumental concept of the lower classes it promoted was perfectly in tune with
the needs of industrial capitalism and only a slightly modified
version of the colonial concept of hierarchy was applied to the
British society itself. The tragedy of colonialism was also the
tragedy of the younger sons, the women, and all 'the etceteras
and and-so-forths' of Britain.

Nobody who wandered among the imperial gravestones, though, pon-
dering the sadness of their separate tragedies, could fail to wonder at
the waste of it all, the young lives thrown away, the useless courage,
the unnecessary partings; and the fading image of Empire, its even
dimmer panoply of flags and battlements, seemed then to be hazed in
a mist of tears, like a grand old march shot through with melancholy,
in a bandstand by the sea.[46]

Secondly and paradoxically, the ideology of colonialism produced a false sense of cultural homogeneity in Britain. This

---

[45] Some of these emphases are compatible with the 'standard' description of the
authoritarian syndrome deriving from the Frankfurt School of Marxists, elaborated
empirically in T. W. Adorno *et al.*, *The Authoritarian Personality*. On the culture of
social Darwinism in Britain, see Raymond Williams, 'Social Darwinism', in
Problems in Materialism and Culture (London: NLB, 1980), pp. 86–102.

[46] James Morris, *Farewell the Trumpets: An Imperial Retreat* (London: Faber and
Faber, 1978), p. 556.

froze social consciousness, discouraging the basic cultural criticism that might have come from growing intellectual sensitivity to the rigid British social classes and subnational divisions, and from the falling quality of life in a quickly industrializing society. Colonialism blurred the lines of social divisions by opening up alternative channels of social mobility in the colonies and by underwriting nationalist sentiments through colonial wars of expansion or through wars with other ambitious European powers seeking a share of colonial glory. The near-total cultural dominance of a small élite in Britain was possible because the society shunted off to the colonies certain indirect expressions of cultural criticism: social deviants unhappy with the social order and buffetted by the stresses within it. I have in mind the criminality which comes from the rage of the oppressed, displaced from the rulers to the co-oppressed.[47] This process was recognized even by some apologists of colonialism. Here is one Carl Siger, speaking of the French experience:

The new countries offer a vast field for individual violent activities which, in the metropolitan countries, would run up against certain prejudices, against a sober and orderly conception of life, and which, in the colonies, have greater freedom to develop and consequently, to affirm their worth. Thus to a certain extent the colonies can serve as. a safety valve for modern society. Even if this were their only value, it would be immense.[48]

The British might not ever have put it that way, but this logic was always implicit in the ruling culture of Britain.

Thirdly, there was what E. M. Forster called the 'undevel-

---

[47] Fanon in his *The Wretched of the Earth* seems to recognize this displacement.

[48] *Essai sur la Colonisation*, Paris, 1907, quoted in Césaire, *Discourse on Colonialism*, p. 20. Césaire also quotes one straight-thinking Renan: 'The regeneration of the inferior or degenerate races by the superior races is part of the providential order of things for humanity. With us, the common man is nearly always a déclassé nobleman, his heavy hand is better suited to handling the sword than the mental tool. Rather than work, he chooses to fight. ... Pour forth this all-consuming activity onto countries which, like China, are crying aloud for foreign conquest. Turn the adventurers who disturb European society into a *ver sacrum*, a horde like those of the Franks, the Lombards, or the Normans, and every man will be in his right role. Nature has made a race of workers, the Chinese race ... ; a race of tillers of the soil, the Negro ... ; a race of masters and soldiers, the European race' (p. 16).

oped heart' in the British which separated them not merely from the Indians but also from each other.[49] This undevelopment came both in the form of isolation of cognition from affect—which often is a trigger to the 'banal' violence of our times—and in the form of a new pathological fit between ideas and feelings. The theory of imperialism did not remain an insulated political position in Britain; it became a religious and ethical theory and an integral part of a cosmology. It not only structured the inner needs of the changing British society but also gave grotesque expression to a 'primitive' religious and social consciousness that had acquired immense military and technological power and was now operating on a global scale. Richard Congreve, Bishop of Oxford, once said, 'God has entrusted India to us to hold it for Him, and we have no right to give it up.'[50] And what Lord John Russel, a future prime minister of Britain, said about Africa applied to India, too. The aim of colonization, he declaimed, was to encourage religious instruction and let the subjects 'partake of the blessings of Christianity'.[51] Both these worthies were articulating not only an imperial responsibility or a national interest but also a felt sense of religious duty. James Morris sums it up neatly. 'Never mind the true motives and methods of imperialism', he says; 'in the days of their imperial supremacy the British genuinely believed themselves to be performing a divine purpose, innocently, nobly, in the name of God and the Queen.'[52] The other side of this sense of religious duty in the rulers was the growing and deliberately promoted sense of a religious duty to be ruled, including a cosmologically rooted political fatalism in some sections of the Indians. Even Bankimchandra Chatter i's novel *Ānandamaṭh* sought to legitimize this duty to be ruled on the basis of a new theory of stages of history.

49 Forster's *A Passage to India* of course examines this separation only in the context of the British society in India.
50 Quoted in K. Bhaskar Rao, *Rudyard Kipling's India* (Norman: University of Oklahama, 1967), p. 26. See an interesting treatment of this moral dimension in Wurgaft, 'Prospero and Caliban', and Mannoni, *Prospero and Caliban*.
51 Quoted in Morris, *Heaven's Command*, pp. 37–8.
52 Morris, *Farewell to Trumpets*, p. 551.

Finally, as Francis Hutchins and Lewis D. Wurgaft have so convincingly argued in the context of India, colonialism encouraged the colonizers to impute to themselves magical feelings of omnipotence and permanence. These feelings became a part of the British selfhood in Britain too. And the society was sold the idea of being an advanced techno-industrial society where science promised to liberate man from his daily drudgery, an advanced culture where human reason and civilized norms had the greatest influence, and—for the sake of the radical internal critics of the society who took to the idea like fish to water—a polity farthest on the road to revolutionary self-actualization. Britannia not only ruled the waves; for its inhabitants and for its many admirers in Europe it also ruled the future of human self-consciousness. (Both British liberalism and the vaunted British insularity were also underwritten by colonialism in important ways. The full-blown theory of colonialism emerged exactly at the time when, for the liberals, Britain had replaced Napoleonic France as the hope of mankind.[53] Once the empire broke down, the liberalism revealed its racist underside. And the famous insularity, too, gave way to wholesale Westernization—Britain also has its own West—and threatened to leave, as Malcolm Muggeridge once said, some sections of Indians as the sole surviving Britons in the world.)

Jacques Ellul has argued that the two major myths of the modern world are science and history.[54] The contours of both these myths, their early 'developmental pathologies', and the magicality associated with them could be found in the dominant cosmology of nineteenth-century Britain.

These cultural pathologies invoked four distinct responses in British society. The more obvious of them were reflected in Rudyard Kipling (1865–1936) and George Orwell (1903–45), the former representing the pathetic self-hatred and ego constriction which went with colonialism, and the latter the relative

[53] Morris, *Heaven's Command*, Chapter 1.
[54] Jacques Ellul, *The New Demons*, trans. C. Edward Hopkin (New York: Seabury Press, 1975), Chapter 4.

sense of freedom and critical morality which were the true
antitheses of colonialism and which one could acquire only by
working through the colonial consciousness. Both came from
direct or indirect exposure to the colonial situation and both
struggled, though in dramatically different ways, with ideas of
authority, responsibility, psychological security, self-esteem,
hierarchy, power and evangelism. The third response was indirect, unselfconscious and overtly apolitical. It was reflected
in the chaotic, individuated, 'pathological' protests against
hyper-masculinity and over-socialization by individuals like
Oscar Wilde and many of the members of the Bloomsbury
group and by aspects of the élite culture in institutions like
Oxford and Cambridge. I have in mind not the formal radical-
ism of a few politically conscious intellectuals, but the half-
articulated protest by more apparently apolitical intellectuals
against the official ideas of normality and dissent gradually
taking over the whole of the culture of Britain.

Lastly, there was the numerically small but psychologically
significant response of many who wholly opted out of their
colonizing society and fought for the cause of India. Some of
them became marginal to the Western life style in the course of
their search for an alternative vision of an ideal society outside
technocratic utopias and outside modernity. One may describe
them as persons searching for a new utopia untouched by any
Hobbesian dream. Such persons as Sister Nivedita, born Mar-
garet Noble (1867–1911), Annie Besant (1847–1933) and Mira
Behn, born Madeleine Slade (1892–1982), found in Indian versions of religiosity, knowledge and social intervention not
merely a model of dissent against their own society, but also
some protection for their search for new models of transcen-
dence, a greater tolerance of androgyny, and a richer meaning
as well as legitimacy for women's participation in social and
political life.[55] More relevant for us however are others like

[55] Cf. Mira Richard's case, briefly touched upon in pp. 94–6, in this volume.
It is also worth noting that many of these women were Irish. I leave it to the
psycho-historians to work out the possible meanings of these relationships between
womanhood, dependency and independence, Anglo-Irish political relationships,
and Catholicism and its greater tolerance for premodern or nonmodern categories
of thought.

C. F. Andrews (1871–1940) who never became marginal to the West, but found a richer meaning for Western Christianity and a new endorsement of traditional Christian virtues in some strands of anti-colonialism in India. India for them was both a place for Christian social intervention and a place which could be a mirror to organized Western Christianity which had become a cat's paw of British imperialism.

I shall very briefly describe the four responses in the rest of this section.

Kipling probably was the most creative builder of the political myths which a colonial power needs to sustain its self-esteem. The psychological co-ordinates of his imperialist ideology have often been the co-ordinates of the West's image of the non-West in our times.

Elsewhere in this book I have described Kipling's early experiences and world view to show that he was something more than a rabid imperialist with an integrated identity. He was, I have argued, a tragic figure seeking to disown in self-hatred an aspect of his self identified with Indianness—which in turn was identified with victimization, ostracism and violence—because of a cruel first encounter with England after an idyllic childhood in India.[56] In this state, Kipling reproduced in his personal life both the painful cultural changes that had taken place in his society and the history of British colonialism in India from Robert Clive to Winston Churchill.

Since about the seventeenth century, the hyper-masculine over-socialized aspects of European personality had been gradually supplanting the cultural traits which had become identified with femininity, childhood, and later on, 'primitivism'. As part of a peasant cosmology, these traits had been valued aspects of a culture not wedded to achievement and productivity. Now they had to be rejected as alien to mainstream European civilization and projected on to the 'low cultures' of Europe and on to the new cultures European civilization encountered. It was as part of this process that the colonies came to be seen as the abode of people childlike and innocent on the one hand, and

[56] See pp. 64–70 below.

devious, effeminate and passive-aggressive on the other. The positive qualities of childlikeness, Kipling argued, were the attributes of the good savages—for instance, the devoted, obedient martial races of India, the Gunga Dins—and those of the good-hearted, patriotic lower classes of Britain supplying the Raj with 'Tommies' who dutifully went to their untimely death in distant lands. Childish or feminine passive-aggression was the attribute of the effete nationalists and fake sahibs or babus drawn from the non-martial races and that of the uninformed, shallow, British liberals supporting the former. It was also the attribute of whatever apparent civilization India, as opposed to the 'savage' Africans, seemed to have.

This was the ultimate meaning of the spirit of colonialism and its civilizing mission mounted on behalf of modernity and progress. Kipling merely produced new myths to consolidate these cultural ideas as a part of his own search for an integrated selfhood. To use an overworked expression of Herbert Marcuse's, it was an instance of internal repression mirroring an externally repressive system. Kipling's idea of the effeminate, passive-aggressive, and 'half-savage–half-child' Indian was more than an Anglo-Indian stereotype: it was an aspect of Kipling's authenticity and Europe's other face.

The *dénouement* for Kipling came in his old age, when his literary success with generations of young readers had very nearly established his superiority over his critics in India as well as in the West. It came when his only son died defending the cause of the Empire Kipling held so dear. Kipling, neither a clear-cut product of the self-confident colonialism of the nineteenth century nor at home with modern wars based on mega-technology and mega-death, was broken. The fear of loss of nurture had always haunted him. The characters in his stories, mostly parentless like Wilde's, sometimes sought that nurture through a reversal of roles: they secured nurture from their wards, from children and from the childlike aliens they befriended or protected. In the process, they presumably ensured for their creator a similar nurture from the children among—and the children in—his readers. That fantasy world

of nurture from below, perhaps compensating loss or depriva-
tion of parental nurture, collapsed with the death of Kipling's
son.

Edmund Wilson sensitively captures the spirit of this Kipling,
broken as much by the imperialism he so admired as by his
self-repression.[57] Wilson does so by quoting the defeated imperialist—lonely, depressed, and fearful of insanity in his old
age:

> I have a dream—a dreadful dream—
> A dream that is near done,
> I watch a man go out of his mind,
> And he is My Mother's Son.

George Orwell's response to the ideology of colonialism was the
antipode of Kipling's; he worked with creative myths that were
direct attempts to reassert some of the values which colonialism
forced one to disown. He clearly sensed that British colonialism
had created the demand for a 'mother culture'—and a production line for colonial rulers—which alienated the colonizers not
only from their political subjects but also from their own selves.
Orwell operated from an anthropocentric, socialist-humanistic
rationalism which never allowed him to develop the full meaning of the continuity between the oppressor and the oppressed.[58]
Nevertheless, he did sense that the subjugation of the ruled also
involved the subjugation of the ruler, that the subjects in the
colonies controlled their rulers as surely as the rulers controlled
their subjects. He also was aware, perhaps to some extent
against himself, that the first kind of control was the more
difficult to defy because it was covert, subtle and involved

[57] Edmund Wilson, 'The Kipling that Nobody Read', in Andrew Rutherford
(ed.), *Kipling's Mind and Art* (Stanford, California: Stanford University Press,
1964), pp. 17–69.

[58] See for instance Orwell's 'Reflections on Gandhi', in Sonia Orwell and Ian
Angus (eds.), *Collected Essays, Journalism and Letters of George Orwell* (London: Secker
and Warburg, 1968), vol. 4, pp. 463–70. Orwell stresses the moral Gandhi and
rejects Gandhi's world view as irrational and anti-humanist and his personality as
aesthetically distasteful. In the same volume however is his 'James Burnham and
the Managerial Revolution', pp. 160–81, which does show an acute sensitivity to
the specific problem of modern oppression which Gandhi attacked.

within-person repression, whereas in the second case, the repression was overt and involved two cultures.

The most telling portrayal of this mutual bondage is in Orwell's 'Shooting an Elephant', an essay which graphically describes some of the anxieties and fears the colonizer lives with.[59] All the themes which can be identified with the present cultural crisis of the West are in the essay: the reification of social bonds through formal, stereotyped, part-object relationships; an instrumental view of nature; created loneliness of the colonizers in the colony through a theory of cultural stratification and exclusivism; an unending search for masculinity and status before the colonized; the perception of the colonized as gullible children who must be impressed with conspicuous machismo (with resultant audience demands binding the colonizer to a given format of 'play'); and the suppression of one's self for the sake of an imposed imperial identity—inauthentic and killing in its grandiosity. What Kipling articulated indirectly through his life and tried to hide through his writings, Orwell articulated openly through his self-aware political analysis.

Orwell was basically a critic of totalitarianism. But those who have read his *Animal Farm* and *Nineteen Eighty-Four* will recognize him also as a critic of the oppression which grows out of ideologies of egalitarianism and progress. It is this part of his self which is relevant to this essay, because much before the modern doctrines of progress came home to roost in the First and the Second Worlds, the colonized societies had to bear their full brunt.

Orwell was the scion of an old, quasi-aristocratic family in decline, with a history of colonial service and slave-owning. Like Kipling, he was born in India and brought up in England. But he left the country of his birth too early to have any memories. He had, thus, a standard English middle-class upbringing. In later life Orwell believed that he had had an oppressive childhood and he wrote about his journey through

[59] George Orwell, *Inside the Whale and Other Essays* (Harmondsworth: Penguin, 1957), pp. 91–100. See also his *Burmese Days* (Harmondsworth: Penguin, 1967).

a tyrannical school that was close to being a 'total' institution. His biographer Bernard Crick however argues that, objectively speaking, Orwell's childhood was not really oppressive after all, that Orwell 'rewrote' his memories to make them compatible with his later concerns.[60] But at the same time, Crick's account itself underscores three themes in Orwell's early life which are linked with the adult Orwell's understanding of oppression and his defiance of the colonial culture in Britain.

First, Orwell grew up in an essentially woman's world with imageries of men as dirty, violent and inferior. Like Kipling he showed an early predilection for a life of the mind; like Kipling, he felt handicapped in a school organized around conflicting ideas of asceticism, sexual (especially homosexual) puritanism, hard work, sportsmanship and hyper-masculinity.[61] Like Kipling again, Orwell was a sensitive, seclusive boy and for that very reason unpopular in his school and subject to bullying. But the end-results of these experiences were very different for Orwell. The ambivalence towards maleness in his early environment deterred him from opting for the reigning culture of hyper-masculinity. He remained in essence an opponent of the patriarchal world view.

Secondly, young Orwell, according to Orwell the autobiographer, learnt early in his life that he was 'in a world where it was *not possible* for him to be good'; that is, 'in a world . . . where the rules were such that it was actually not possible . . . to keep them.'[62] This probably included the specific lesson that the inability to be good applied especially to the weak. All this can be explained away as a 'screen memory', as Crick seems to do, but it could be also read as a belief rooted in experience. Orwell was a bed-wetter, and had to learn to live with humiliation and corporal punishment in school for his 'crime'. Victorian morality taught him to recognize bed-wetting as wicked, but

[60] Bernard Crick, *George Orwell, A Life* (Boston: Little, Brown, 1980), especially Chapters 1 and 2. It is not clear why Crick stresses this point because Orwell *does* admit it (pp. 344, 347).

[61] George Orwell, 'Such, Such Were the Joys', in *Collected Essays*, vol. 4, pp. 330–69, see particularly pp. 351–3, 359.

[62] Ibid., p. 334.

the wickedness was outside his control. 'Sin was not necessarily something that you did; it might be something that happened to you.'[63]

Third, it was in school that Orwell had the first intimation of a principle which took him, by his own admission, another twenty years to realize: 'the weak in a world governed by the strong' must 'break the rules, or perish.' The weak, he was to claim, had 'the right to make a different set of rules for themselves.'[64] Unless they had the 'instinct to survive', they had to accept the world in which 'there were the strong, who deserved to win, and there were the weak who deserved to lose and always did lose, everlastingly.'[65]

Strange though it may sound, Orwell could have been, given the 'right' values, one of Kipling's heroes. He had the right approach to the 'natives' as well as to the English lower classes: deep empathy without total identification, a sense of moral responsibility, and an unencumbered spirit of the kind which enabled one to do the dirty work of one's time. But Orwell put this approach to a different use. He became a critic of the dominant, middle-class culture of modern Britain which had found in imperialism its final fulfilment.

The third form of internal response to colonialism protected the more feminine aspects of the British self through 'psycho-pathological'—and 'criminal'—modes of self-expression in a few confined geographical and psychological spaces such as Oxbridge and Bloomsbury and in persons in conflict about their sexual identities and seeking to make an indirect ideological issue out of the conflicts. Almost all these persons were unaware that their inner drives were a joint political statement as well as the elements of a common private conflict. Nevertheless, their personal lives and the ambience of their interpersonal relationships set apart such non-political figures as Oscar Wilde (1854–1900), G. E. Moore (1873–1958), John Maynard Keynes (1883–1946), Lytton Strachey (1880–1932), Virginia Woolf (1882–1941), Somerset Maugham (1874–1965), E. M. Forster

[63] Ibid., p. 334.   [64] Ibid., pp. 362–3.   [65] Ibid., pp. 359, 361.

(1879–1970) and W. H. Auden (1907–73) as living protests against the world view associated with colonialism.

Psychoanalyst Lawrence Kubie has explored in some detail the search for bisexuality that characterized gifted individuals like Virginia Woolf and the anguish that was associated with that search.[66] This anguish was sharpened in a cultural context that was trying to disown its own recessive traditions of androgyny and the psychological correlates of the biological fact of human bisexuality.[67] 'The ideology of higher sodomy', aestheticism and neo-Hellenism to which many creative persons subscribed in nineteenth and twentieth century Britain cannot be explained without reference to the way British society had devalued femininity as low-status, contaminating and antisocial, and rejected the presence of femininity in man as virtually the negation of all humanness. What the colonial culture was doing in India by stressing the antonymy between *puruṣatva* and *klībatva* had its collateral in the struggle to further consolidate the dominance of the principle of hyper-masculinity in Britain. Colonialism only helped marginalize, using the popular British sexual stereotypes, the strands of consciousness in Britain protesting against this antonymy.

Let me give the example of a remarkably creative person who was apparently far removed from the world of British-Indian politics, Oscar Wilde. Richard Ellmann's recent essay on Wilde's life at once reveals the extent to which Wilde's sexuality was a cultural phenomenon and a statement of protest.[68] The Marquess of Queensberry, the vindictive father of Wilde's lover

---

[66] Lawrence Kubie, 'The Drive to Become Both Sexes' *Psychoanalytic Quarterly*, 1974, 43(3), pp. 349–426.

[67] See also the autobiography of Noël Coward, *Future Indefinite* (London: Heinemann, 1954), for a flavour of how wit and pleasantness was often used to hide the pain and loneliness of sexual deviation within the mould of social acceptability and popularity. For a discussion of 'the structure of feeling' which interlinked critiques of existing man–woman relationship, attempts to relate to lower classes, anti-imperialism and anti-militarism, see Raymond Williams, 'The Bloomsbury Fraction', *Problems in Materialism and Culture*, pp. 148–69. Williams also provides a vague clue to the nature of the relationship between depth psychology and the Bloomsbury syndrome.

[68] Richard Ellmann, 'A Late Victorian Love Affair', *New York Review of Books*, 1977, 24(13), pp. 6–10.

Bossie (Lord Alfred Douglas) was not merely a flat-footed conservative, but a culturally typical counterplayer to Wilde's atypical sexual identity. Both Wilde and his lover saw themselves as the negation of the staid Marquess who sought constant endorsement of not only his but his culture's masculine self. As the inventor of the Queensberry rules of competitive boxing, it is this endorsement which the Marquess symbolically sought by defining and demanding rule-bound violence and conformity to that ultimate virtue of aggressive British masculinity, sportsmanship.[69] And this is the endorsement Wilde tried to deny him. Wilde's younger son, Vyvyan Holland, was to later write that Wilde had a 'horror of conventionality' and that this contributed to his destruction by his society.[70] He failed to recognize that imperialism was based on the pathology of existing conventionality and commonsense; it sought its legitimacy by selling the idea of a moral civilization based on these two elements of British folk culture. By defying conventionality—particularly stereotyped definitions of sexual norms —Wilde threatened, however indirectly, a basic postulate of the colonial attitude in Britain.

It is well known that Wilde's homosexuality would have been 'forgiven' had he been more discreet about it; had he, for instance, not instituted criminal proceedings against the Marquess. Victorian England was willing to tolerate Wilde's sexual identity as long as it was accepted as a part of the life style of a marginal sect and not openly flaunted.

But by demonstratively using his homosexuality as a cultural ideology, Wilde threatened to sabotage his community's dominant self-image as a community of well-defined men, with clear-cut man–woman relationships. What the élite culture of England could not tolerate was his blatant deviation from rigidly defined sexual roles in a society which, unknown to the hyper-aesthete Wilde, was working out the political

---

[69] Geoffrey Gorer, 'The British National Character in the Twentieth Century', *The Annals of the American Academy of Political and Social Sciences*, no. 370, March 1967, pp. 74–81, see especially pp. 77–8.

[70] Quoted in H. Montgomery Hyde, *Oscar Wilde* (London: Methuen, 1976), p. 136.

meanings of these definitions in a colony thousands of miles away.

Oscar Wilde 'childishly' defied respectability in yet another sphere. By stressing this part of Wilde's ideology, Ellmann, a literary critic, allows me to conceptualize the essentially apolitical Wilde as an unself-aware, but more or less complete, critic of the political culture which sired colonialism.[71] Wilde rejected Matthew Arnold's dictum: 'The aim of criticism is to see the object as in itself it really is.' To him the aim of criticism was to see the object as it really was not. This may be seen as the other side of the old maxim, art for art's sake, but it could also be read, as Ellmann himself says, as an earlier version of Picasso's faith: art is 'what nature is not'. In that form it becomes an early critique of over-socialized thinking, of the kind later ventured by Theodor Adorno and Herbert Marcuse. The art which defies the existent is the art which is subversive; it 'undermines things as they are.' Thus, Wilde's admiration for historians who defy history:

He celebrates those historians who impose dominion upon fact instead of surrendering to it. Later he was to say much more boldly, 'The one duty we owe to history is to rewrite it.' It is part of his larger conception that the one duty (or better, whim) we owe nature, reality, or the world, is to reconstruct it.[72]

Wilde, everything said, was a marginal man. His philosophy of life, too, was peripheral to his society. Neither his sexual deviance nor his critiques of everyday life and history made sense to the mainstream culture of Britain. Appropriately, the characters he created for his plays and stories were parentless.[73] They were not burdened by close authority and thus by any passionate conflict with such authority. The humour these characters produced arose out of distant defiance rather than proximate rebellion. Perhaps it is now time for us to turn to criticisms of Western culture which defied conventional masculinity and normal history as parts of a more articulate,

[71] Richard Ellmann, 'The Critic as Artist as Wilde', *Encounter*, July 1967, pp. 29–37.

[72] Ibid., pp. 30–1.   [73] Ibid., p. 30.

culturally legitimate, ideology. In other words, I shall now
discuss a mode of dissent which had parents.

Charles Freer Andrews, revered in India and forgotten in
England, was born into an inheritance of religion and non-
conformity.[74] Like Orwell, he was his mother's favourite and,
like both Kipling and Orwell, his relationship with his father,
a minister of the Catholic Apostolic Church, was distant.
Andrews' childhood was deeply influenced by religious myths
and imageries, and he was also exposed to more than the
normal quota of classical literature. He was later to describe
his early home life as 'a kind of backwater into which the
current of modern thought has not been allowed to enter.'[75]
Again like Kipling and Orwell, he was miserable in his school,
partly because of the burden of his studies, but more so because,
as a delicate, over-protected boy he was surrounded by older,
bigger and 'coarser' boys whose object of homosexual attention
he became. Andrews' response to them was not perhaps entirely
passive and, throughout his life, he was to remember these
experiences as 'an evil form of impurity' in him. Hugh Tinker,
certainly not an overly psychological biographer, describes the
consequences as follows:

> Charlie was never to have a girl friend, and the enormity of this 'im-
> purity' was to be buried deep in his psyche. Perhaps it was at school
> that he subconsciously turned, or was turned away from the possibility
> of the physical love of a woman. For some years there was an emo-
> tional struggle at school, and though as he grew older he mastered
> the situation, the sense of guilt remained.[76]

Andrews may not have been easy with conventional hetero-
sexuality but in spite of all his neurasthenia and nervous
activism, he was always easy with children. Whether it was
this combination that helped him see through the colonial
ideology or not, he was to become the one person who, to
many of his friends, 'was an Indian at heart, at the same time

---

[74] Hugh Tinker, *The Ordeal of Love: C. F. Andrews and India* (New Delhi: Oxford
University Press, 1979), p. 1.
[75] Ibid., p. 5.   [76] Ibid., p. 4.

a true Englishman.'[77] It is thus that he bridged the classical universalism of Rabindranath Tagore and the folk-based, critical traditionalism of Gandhi. He saw both as valid alternatives to the modernism which informed colonial ideology and, though he probably found Tagore easier to understand, he based his critique of British colonialism, following Gandhi, on critical Christian ethics. (He would have certainly rejected the apolitical, non-critical traditionalism of some contemporary Christian missionaries, as he would have rejected its more impressive and touching version in someone like Mother Teresa today. He would have considered such anti-politics unacceptable.[78]) Predictably, when in India, Andrews adopted many Indian and specifically Hindu social customs—in dress, food and social relations—but he also took care to see that nobody mistook him for a lapsed Christian. He even took pains during his last years to ensure a proper Christian burial for himself. Evidently, he owed his social and political activism not merely to his Indianized self, but also to his non-modern Western traditions. It is a comment on modern theories of dissent that the Westerner who perhaps came closest to the Indian cause in two hundred years of British colonial history operated on the basis of religious traditions, not on that of a secular ideology.

In a moment of terrible defeatism Vivekananda had said that the salvation of the Hindus lay in three Bs: beef, biceps and Bhagvad-Gītā. The nationalist-chemist P. C. Ray, too, allegedly expressed similar sentiments once. Andrews, if he had come across such proposals, would have found them painful. He recognized the nexus between capitalism, imperialism and Christianity, in spite of his limited intellectual repertoire and his simple theology.[79] Nevertheless, his Christianity demanded

[77] M. K. Gandhi, quoted in Pyarelal, *Mahatma Gandhi: The Last Phase* (Ahmedabad: Navajivan Publishing House, 1958), vol. 2, p. 100.

[78] This I say in spite of his liking for Albert Schweitzer (Tinker, *The Ordeal of Love*, p. 206) whose subtle moral and cultural arrogance the simple Andrews was unlikely to notice.

[79] C. F. Andrews, *Christ and Labour* (London: Student Christian Movement, 1923); and *What I Owe to Christ* (London: Hodder Stoughton, 1932).

from the Hindus not a masculine Christianity masquerading as Hindu nationalism. His Christianity sought to authenticate Gandhi's faith, enumerated in his sixteen-point thesis, that the East and West could—and did—meet outside the bounds of modernity.[80] It was modern Britain Andrews disowned, not the traditional West. When Gandhi described him as an Indian at heart and a true Englishman, it remained unstated that it was by being a true Englishman that Andrews became an Indian.

My account of the responses to colonialism in Britain—I find after having written it—differs from my account of the Indian responses in one respect. In the case of the Indians I seem to have stressed texts and myths; for the Westerners, persons. Is this accidental? Or is this an unwilling acknowledgement of the different ways in which cultures can be described? Are some cultures primarily organized around historical time intersecting with life-histories, and others around the timeless time of myths and texts? One of the following sections may provide a partial answer to these questions.

VI

The most creative response to the perversion of Western culture, however, came, as it must, from its victims. It was colonial India, still preserving something of its androgynous cosmology and style, which ultimately produced a transcultural protest against the hyper-masculine world view of colonialism, in the form of Gandhi. Gandhi's authenticity as an Indian should not blind us to the way his idiom cut across the cultural barriers between Britain and India, and Christianity and Hinduism. Albeit a non-Westerner, Gandhi always tried to be a living symbol of the other West. Not only did he sense and 'use' the fundamental predicament of British culture caught in the hinges of imperial responsibility and subjecthood in victory, but he implicitly defined his ultimate goal as the liberation of

[80] Gandhi, quoted in T. K. Mahadevan, *Dvija* (New Delhi: East-West Affiliated Press, 1977), pp. 118–19.

the British from the history and psychology of British colonialism. The moral and cultural superiority of the oppressed was not an empty slogan to him.

That is why Gandhi's spirited search for the other culture of Britain, and of the West, was an essential part of his theory of salvation for India. It is true that 'Gandhi was a living antithesis set up against the thesis of the English',[81] but that antithesis was latent in the English, too. All through his adulthood, Gandhi's closest friend was an English cleric devoted not only to the cause of Indian freedom but also to a softer version of Christianity. C. F. Andrews was to Gandhi what Thomas Mann had been to Sigmund Freud: an affirmation of the marginalized reflective strain that must underlie—or, to protect one's own sanity and humanity, must be presumed to underlie—every 'homogeneous' culture that goes rabid. (That this may not be reduced to a merely moral posture in circumstances in which shared madness establishes its domination over history is best shown by Gene Sharpe's description of a successful peaceful resistance against the Nazi state in wartime Berlin.[82]) Similarly, Gandhi's partiality for some of the Christian hymns and Biblical texts was more than the symbolic gesture of a Hindu towards a minority religion in India. It was also an affirmation that, at one plane, some of the recessive elements of Christianity were perfectly congruent with elements of Hindu and Buddhist world views and that the battle he was fighting for the minds of men was actually a universal battle to rediscover the softer side of human nature, the so-called non-masculine self of man relegated to the forgotten zones of the Western self-concept.

What was the constituency he was appealing to? Was it only a lunatic fringe or an ineffective minority? I suspect that there was in Gandhi not only a sophisticated ethical sensitivity but also political and psychological shrewdness. Here is, for in-

---

[81] Rollo May, *Power and Innocence: A Search for the Sources of Violence* (New York: Delta, 1972), p. 112.

[82] Gene Sharpe, *The Politics of Nonviolent Action*, vol. 1 (Boston: Porter Sargent, 1973), pp. 87–90.

stance, a description of an aspect of British national character which the reader, if brought up on ideas of Indian and particularly Gandhian pacifism and Western aggressiveness, might find interesting:

With the exception of the anomalous members of the lower working class (who never came to the colonies in large numbers), the English are preoccupied with the control of their own aggression, the avoidance of aggression from others, and the prevention of the emergence of aggressive behaviour in their children . . . In the English middle and upper classes this control of aggression would appear to have been a major component in their character for several centuries. In the context of games this control of aggression is called 'sportsmanship', a concept which the English introduced into much of the rest of the world. One aspect of 'sportsmanship' is controlling physical aggression by rules. . . . The other aspect of 'sportsmanship' is the acceptance of the outcome unaggressively, neither taunting the vanquished nor showing resentment against the victor. This concept of 'sportsmanship' has long been metaphorically extended from games to almost all situations of rivalry or competition; the reputation of being a 'good sport' is one that is very highly valued by the majority of the English.[83]

Against this observation I want to offset the view of Nirad C. Chaudhuri, an internal critic of the Indic civilization, even though he would be rejected out-of-hand by many as hopelessly anti-Indian and as a lobbyist for the West in the East.

The current belief is that the Hindus are a peace-loving and non-violent people, and this belief has been fortified by Gandhism. In reality few communities have been more warlike and fond of bloodshed. . . . About twenty-five words in an inscription of Asoka have succeeded in almost wholly suppressing the thousands in the rest of the epigraphy and the whole of Sanskrit literature which bear testimony to the incorrigible militarism of the Hindus. Their political history is made up of bloodstained pages. . . . Between this unnecessary proclamation of non-violence in the third century B.C. and its reassertion, largely futile, in the twentieth century by Mahatma Gandhi, there is not *one word* of non-violence in the theory and practice of statecraft by the Hindus.[84]

[83] Gorer, 'The British National Character', p. 77.

[84] Nirad C. Chaudhuri, *The Continent of Circe* (London: Chatto and Windus, 1965), pp. 98–9. A number of social scientists, too, have noticed that the aggressive needs repeatedly top the list among needs projected in projective, particularly thematic, tests and many of them have identified aggression as the

Mine is not an attempt to substitute the existing stereotypes of the British ruler and Indian subject with the help of two partisan observers. What I am saying is that Gandhi's non-violence was probably not a one-sided morality play. Nor was it purely a matter of humane Hindus versus the inhuman Britons. The shrewd Bania, a practical idealist, had correctly seen that, at some levels of national consciousness in Britain, there was near-perfect legitimacy for the political methodology he was forging. On the other hand, he knew well that he would have to fight hard in India to establish his version of non-violence as 'true' Hinduism or as the central core of Hinduism. After all, Gandhi himself said that he had borrowed his idea of non-violence not from the sacred texts of India but from the Sermon on the Mount. In the 150 years of British rule prior to Gandhi, no significant social reformer or political leader had tried to give centrality to non-violence as a major Hindu or Indian virtue. The closest anyone came to it was Rammohun Roy with his concept of *dayā* or mercy. Many years before Gandhi, Swami Vivekananda had sarcastically said that the British had, following the 'real' injunctions of the classical Indian texts, excelled in their this-worldly, hedonic, manly pursuits, while the Indians, foolishly following the 'true' injunctions of Christianity, had become their passive, life-denying, feminine subjects.[85] It is not relevant whether Vivekananda's reading of Christianity and Hinduism was right. The important point is that Gandhi made a different use of the same awareness.

It was in this sense that Gandhi wanted to liberate the British as much as he wanted to liberate Indians. The panicky, self-imposed captivity of the dominant or ruling groups in their self-made oppressive systems, for the sake of values which Chaim Shatan has recently called bogus honour and bogus

---

Indian's major conflict area. For details see Ashis Nandy and Sudhir Kakar, 'Culture and Personality', in Udai Pareekh (ed.), *Research in Psychology* (Bombay: Popular Prakashan, 1980), pp. 136–67.

[85] Vivekananda, *Prācya o Pāścātya* (Almora: Advaita Ashrama, 1898). This aspect of Vivekananda comes out also from Sudhir Kakar's interpretation of Vivekananda in *The Inner World: Childhood and Society in India* (New Delhi: Oxford University Press, 1977), pp. 160–81.

manliness, is something which he never failed to notice or use.[86]

To put this awareness to political use, he challenged first the ideology of biological stratification acting as a homologue of —and legitimacy for—political inequality and injustice. As already noted, the colonial culture's ordering of sexual identities assumed that

$$Puruṣatva > Nārītva > Klībatva$$

That is, manliness is superior to womanliness, and womanliness in turn to femininity in man. I have also pointed out that the first Indian response to this was to accept the ordering by giving a new salience to Kṣatriyahood as true Indianness. To beat the colonizers at their own game and to regain self-esteem as Indians and as Hindus, many sensitive minds in India did what the adolescent Gandhi at the ontogenetic level had tried to do symbolically with the help of a Muslim friend:[87] they sought a hyper-masculinity or hyper-Kṣatriyahood that would make sense to their fellow-countrymen (specially to those exposed to the majesty of the Raj) and to the colonizers.

But in an unorganized plural society, with a tradition of only parochial, not absolute, legitimacy for warriorhood, such Dionysian games with the colonizers were doomed. This is what the Bengali, Panjabi and Maharashtrian terrorists found out to their own cost during the early part of this century. They had isolated themselves from the society even more than the British when Gandhi entered Indian politics in the nineteen-twenties.

Gandhi's solution was different. He used two orderings, each of which could be invoked according to the needs of the situation. The first, borrowed intact from the great and little traditions of saintliness in India, and also probably from the doctrine

[86] Chaim F. Shatan, 'Bogus Manhood and Bogus Honor: Surrender and Transfiguration in the United States Marine Corps', *Psychoanalytic Review*, 1977, 64(4), pp. 585–610.

[87] On the young Gandhi's attempt to work out or pursue at the personal level the macho model to its logical absurdity see the sensitive account of Erik H. Erikson, *Gandhi's Truth: On the Origins of Militant Non-Violence* (New York: Norton, 1969).

of power through divine bi-unity in some of the *vāmāchārī* or left-handed sects, was as follows:

$$\text{Androgyny} > \frac{Puruṣatva}{Nārītva}$$

That is, manliness and womanliness are equal, but the ability to transcend the man–woman dichotomy is superior to both, being an indicator of godly and saintly qualities. To do this Gandhi had to ignore the traditional devaluation of some forms of androgyny in his culture.

Gandhi's second ordering was invoked specifically as a methodological justification for the anti-imperialist movement, first in South Africa and then in India. It went as follows:

$$Nārītva > Puruṣatva > Kāpuruṣatva$$

That is, the essence of femininity is superior to that of masculinity, which in turn is better than cowardice or, as the Sanskrit expression would have it, failure of masculinity. Though the ordering is not inconsistent with some interpretations of Indian traditions, when stated in such a fashion it acquires a new play. This is because the first relationship (*nārītva > puruṣatva*) often applies more directly to the transcendental and the magical, whereas the second relationship (*puruṣatva > kāpuruṣatva*) is a more general, everyday principle. Perhaps the conjunction of the two sets makes available the magical power of the feminine principle of the cosmos to the man who chooses to defy his cowardice by owning to his feminine self.

There are a few implied meanings in these relationships. These meanings were culturally defined and, therefore, 'assumed' by Gandhi, but could be missed by an outside observer. First, the concept of *nārītva*, so repeatedly stressed by Gandhi nearly fifty years before the woman's liberation movement began, represented more than the dominant Western definition of womanhood. It included some traditional meanings of womanhood in India, such as the belief in a closer conjunction between power, activism and femininity than between power, activism and masculinity. It also implied the belief that the feminine principle is a more powerful, dangerous and uncontrollable principle in the cosmos than the male principle. But even more central to this concept of womanhood was the traditional Indian belief in the primacy of maternity over conjugality in feminine identity. This belief specified that woman as an object and source of sexuality was inferior to woman as source of motherliness and *caritas*. Gandhi's fear of human sexuality, whatever its psychodynamic explanation in Gandhi's personal history, was perfectly consistent with this reading of Indian culture.

Second, while the dominant principle in Gandhian praxis is non-violence or avoidable violence, an implicit subsidiary principle is what K. J. Shah calls unavoidable violence. The principle of non-violence gives men access to protective maternity and by implication, to the godlike state of *ardhanārīśvara*, a god half-man, half-woman. But given the cultural meaning of *nāritva*, non-violence also gives men access to the powerful, active, maternal principle of the cosmos, magically protective and carrying the intimations of an oceanic and utopian beatitude. Along the same continuum, courage—what Lloyd and Susanne Rudolph call Gandhi's new courage[88]—allows one to rise above cowardice or *kāpuruṣatva* and became a 'man', on the way to becoming the authentic man who admits his drive to become both sexes. This courage is not definitionally wedded to violence as in Kṣatriyahood, but it may involve unavoidable violence under some circumstances, particularly in circumstances where the alternative is passive tolerance of injustice, inequality and oppression—willing victimhood and acceptance of the secondary gains of victimhood—which are all seen as worse than violence.

In sum, Gandhi was clear in his mind that activism and courage could be liberated from aggressiveness and recognized as perfectly compatible with womanhood, particularly maternity. Whether this position fully negated the Kṣatriya world view or not, it certainly negated the very basis of the colonial culture. The colonial culture depended heavily on Western

[88] Lloyd and Susanne Rudolph, *The Modernity of Tradition* (Chicago: University of Chicago Press, 1966), part 2.

cosmology, with its built-in fears about losing potency through the loss of activism and the ability to be violent. I have avoided discussing here the fantasies which underlie these fears—fantasies of rape and counter-rape, seduction and counter-seduction, castration and counter-castration—which have accompanied the Western concept of manhood whenever Western man has gone beyond his narrow cultural borders to civilize, populate or self-improve. (The depth of this linkage between activism and aggression in parts of the Western world is evident from the fact that the West's major ethnopsychology, Freudian psychoanalysis, locates the source of all activism and the concern with power in the instinctual patterning of aggression.)

VII

> The past in history varies with the present, rests upon the present, is the present. . . . There are not two worlds—the world of past happenings and the world of our present knowledge of those past events—there is only one world, and it is a world of present experience.
>
> Michael Oakeshott[89]

Gandhi's reply to the colonial homology between childhood and political subjugation was indirect. He rejected history and affirmed the primacy of myths over historical chronicles. He thereby circumvented the unilinear pathway from primitivism to modernity, and from political immaturity to political adulthood, which the ideology of colonialism would have the subject society and the 'child races' walk.[90] This was his way of grappling with colonial racism, a racism at least one psychiatrist has diagnosed as 'a historical ill, a disorder of the historical self'

[89] Michael Oakeshott, *Experience and its Modes* (Cambridge: Cambridge University Press, 1966), pp. 107-8. Oakeshott's classical conservatism is of course totally oblivious of the critical functions this orientation to history can be made to play. For an implicit awareness of those functions one might have to go back to a politically schizophrenic personality like Martin Heidegger in the modern Western tradition.

[90] As already noted, the equation between childhood and primitivism received powerful support from psychoanalytic ethnography. In Freud's own lifetime, some of his followers were busy studying primitive cultures which supposedly displayed all the characteristics of childhood.

which 'reveals the fullness of that self even as it reveals its inadequacies'.[91]

(There *was* a direct component in Gandhi's defiance of the ideology of adulthood, but it was relatively trivial. Not only did every Westerner and Westernized Indian who came in touch with Gandhi refer at least once to his child's smile, his admirers and detractors dutifully found him childlike and childish respectively. His 'infantile' obstinacy and tendency to tease, his 'immature' attacks on the modern world and its props, his 'juvenile' food fads and symbols like the spinning wheel—all were viewed as planks of a political platform which defied conventional ideas of adulthood.[92] One could offset these oddities against Bruno Bettelheim's view that under oppression, when survival is at stake, there is regression to infantilism. And against Lionel Trilling's observation, in the context of India, that 'generations of subjection can diminish the habit of dignity and teach grown men the strategy of the little child.'[93] An enterprising psychoanalyst probably could even be persuaded to argue that Gandhi's style of leadership was, in retrospect, a natural corollary of the culture of oppression with which his people lived. For the moment, however, I shall stress the other part of the story where a specific political position became in Gandhi a point of convergence between immediate social needs and metaphysical defiance.)

Gandhi's position on history was based on three assumptions, two of them derived from the traditional Indian orientations to time.[94] The first of these two was the salience given by

---

[91] Joel Kovel, *White Racism: A Psychohistory* (London: Allen Lane, 1970), p. 232.

[92] Ashis Nandy, 'From Outside the Imperium: Gandhi's Cultural Critique of the "West" ', *Alternatives*, 1981, 7(2), pp. 171–94.

[93] Bruno Bettelheim, *Surviving and Other Essays* (New York: Alfred A. Knopf, 1979); Lionel Trilling, 'A Passage to India (1943)', in Malcolm Bradbury (ed.), *E. M. Forster: A Passage to India* (London: Macmillan, 1970), pp. 77–92, especially p. 80.

[94] For an excellent detailed analysis of the traditional Indian concept of time as it relates to authority and change, see Madhav Deshpande, 'History, Change and Permanence: A Classical Indian Perspective', in Gopal Krishna (ed.), *Contributions to South Asian Studies*, vol. 1 (New Delhi: Oxford University Press, 1979), pp. 1–28.

Indian culture to myth as a structured fantasy which, in its dynamic of the here-and-the-now, represents what in another culture would be called the dynamic of history. In other words, the diachronic relationships of history are mirrored in the synchronic relationship of myths and are fully reproducible from the latter if the rules of transformation are known. In Gandhi, the specific orientation to myth became a more general orientation to public consciousness. Public consciousness was not seen as a causal product of history but as related to history non-causally through memories and anti-memories. If for the West the present was a special case of an unfolding history, for Gandhi as a representative of traditional India history was a special case of an all-embracing permanent present, waiting to be interpreted and reinterpreted. (This also indirectly coped with the subsidiary homology between old age and Indian civilization but, for the moment, I shall let that pass.)

Even to the critics of industrial capitalism in the West, history was a linear process sometimes with an implied cycle underlying it. Marx, for instance, following the Judaeo-Christian cosmology, conceived of history somewhat as follows:

Prehistory proper (ahistorical primitive communism)	→	Objective stage-bound history (class struggle)	→	End of history (class-less adult communism, based on scientific history)
		↓ ↑ False history as a part of false consciousness (History as ideology)		

Gandhi, however, was a product of a society which conceptualized the past, as a possible means of reaffirming or altering the present:

| Past as a special case of present | → | Fractured present (competing pasts) | → | Remaking of present including past | → | New Past |

From such a viewpoint, the past can be an authority but the nature of the authority is seen as shifting, amorphous and amenable to intervention. Mircea Eliade puts it thus:

While a modern man, though regarding himself as the result of the course of universal history, does not feel obliged to know the whole of it, the man of the archaic societies is not only obliged to remember mythical history but also to *re-enact* a large part of it periodically. It is here that we find the greatest difference between the man of the archaic societies and modern man: the irreversibility of events, which is the characteristic trait of History for the latter, is not a fact to the former. . . .[95]

This is of course a less colourful way of paraphrasing T. S. Eliot in *Burnt Norton*:

> Time present and time past
> Are both perhaps present in time future,
> And time future is contained in time past.
> If all time is eternally present
> All time is [un]redeemable.

Borrowing from psychoanalysis, Jürgen Habermas in another context uses the expression 'future-oriented memories' to describe the means through which one breaks the power of the past over the present.[96] Some strands of Indian culture would find this fully acceptable. But they would formulate the consequences of such a view differently. The Indian's past is always open, whereas his future is so only to the extent that it is a rediscovery or renewal.[97] For Freud, as for Marx, ill health follows from history; health either from the present or from the future. The psychoanalyst, like the Marxist historian, is an expert who anticipates the self's capacity to bare, and live with, the repressed other history which creates the crucial disjunction between the past and the present. For the Indian folk 'historian' —the *bhāṭ*, *cāraṇ*, or the *kathākār* for instance—there can be no real disjunction between the past and the present. If ill health follows from the past, health too follows from the past. The idea

---

[95] Mircea Eliade, *Myths, Rites, Symbols*, Wendell C. Beane and William G. Doty (eds.) (New York: Harper Colophon Books, 1976), vol. 1, p. 5.

[96] Jürgen Habermas, 'Moral Development and Ego Identity', in *Communication and the Evolution of Society*, trans. Thomas McCarthy (London: Heinemann, 1979), pp. 69–94.

[97] For a brief discussion of this attitude from a psychological point of view, see my *Alternative Sciences: Creativity and Authenticity in Two Indian Scientists* (New Delhi: Allied, 1980), Chapter 1.

of 'determination' could apply to the present or to the future, as the notorious Indian concept of fatalism implies; in the past there are always open choices.

Past as present	→	Fractured present	→	Remade past	→	New past
↓						↓
Determined future (Indian fatalism)						Alternative determined future (new 'fatalism')

While this position does not fully negate history and in fact anticipates a number of fashionable post-Gandhian philosophies of history and interpretations of myths as history, the Gandhian position does make a subsidiary anti-historical assumption that, because they faithfully contain history, because they are contemporary and, unlike history, are amenable to intervention, myths are the essence of a culture, history being at best superfluous and at worst misleading. Gandhi implicitly assumed that history or *itihāsa* was one-way traffic, a set of myths about past time or the *atīt*, built up as independent variables which limit human options and pre-empt human futures. Myths, on the other hand, allow one access to the processes which constitute history at the level of the here-and-the-now. Consciously acknowledged as the core of a culture, they widen instead of restricting human choices. They allow one to remember in an anticipatory fashion and to concentrate on undoing aspects of the present rather than avenging the past. (Myths widen human choices also by resisting co-optation by the uniformizing world view of modern science. In spite of recent attempts to show the rationality of the savage mind *à la* Lévi-Strauss, the savage mind itself has remained on the whole unconcerned about its own rationality. Both the science of myth and the scientific status of the myth continue to be a predominantly modern concern. In this sense, too, the affirmation of ahistoricity is an affirmation of the dignity and autonomy of non-modern peoples.)

The reverse of the same logic, however, is that myths can be analysed, traced or reduced to history as the dominant tradition of Western social analysis had tried to do throughout modern times. History here is seen as the reality, the myth being a flawed, irrational fairy tale produced by 'unconscious' history, meant for savages and children. The core of such a concept of time—produced in the West for the first time after the demise of medievalism—consists in the emphasis on causes rather than on structures (on 'why' rather than 'what'), on progress and evolution as opposed to self-realization-in-being, and on the rationality of adjustment to historical reality (pragmatics) and of change through constant dramatic action (rather than on the rationality of a fundamentally critical attitude towards earlier interpretations and change through only critical interventions and new interpretations). For the modern West, and for those influenced by its concept of time, history itself is a chronology of good and bad actions and their causes, and every revolution is a disjunction in time which must be either protected against counter-revolutions or reduced to the stature of a false 'coming' on the way to a real revolution.

The subsidiary assumption of the second approach is that the cultures living by myths are ahistorical and thus, representatives of an earlier, second-rate social consciousness. Historical societies are the true representatives of mature human self-consciousness and, therefore, their constructions of the ahistorical societies are more valid scientifically than those of these societies themselves. The latter must act out their ahistorical fates as understood by those who are historians to the world.

This is the paradigm of the adult–child relationship which was challenged in Gandhian theory as well as practice.[98] This

---

[98] It was at the level of practice that Gandhi introduced into Indian concepts of childhood and child-rearing something analogous to the concept of original sin. It is a moot psychological point whether, without this distortion of the Indian tradition of childhood (see Sudhir Kakar's 'Childhood in India: Traditional Ideals and Contemporary Reality', *International Social Science Journal*, 1979, 31(3), pp. 444–56), Gandhi personally could have given such a centrality to the concept of *sevā* or service in the public sphere and to the idea of intervention in life situations for which there was very little place in the high cultures of India. Gandhi's concept of *sevā* was essentially reparative; it was born of his own personal experiences, which partly underwrote a Western-style solution of his Oedipal conflicts. As a result, Gandhi built his concept of political and social work on an

was done in two ways: by reaffirming the language of continuity and by re-emphasizing the language of self.

The language of continuity took advantage of the deep ambivalence towards disjunction in the ideology of modernity. Modernity seeks to locate all 'true' creativity, including creative social action, in clear-cut breaks with the past. Yet, paradoxically, it strives hard to locate each such break in history. For instance, the rhetoric of revolution not only undervalues anything which is insufficiently disjunctive with the past; it positively disvalues reformism as a hindrance to revolution. At the same time, the effort of every modern history of revolutions and every revolutionary thought is to place all 'true' or 'false' revolutions in history. No explanation of, or call for, a revolution is complete unless it has spelt out the historical continuities which has or could lead to a revolution or would explain its career line.

The language of continuity re-legitimized the under-emphasis on disjunction in the Indian world view. It recognized that exactly as the language of revolution hid within it the message of continuity, the language of continuity too had a latent message of disjunction. Indian culture emphasized continuities so much that even major breaks with the past passed as minor reforms, till the full implications of the break became evident after decades or centuries, when the metaphors of continuity and permanence could no longer hide the fundamental changes that had already taken place in the culture. (The Bhakti movement is a reasonably good example of the process being described.) It therefore did not ultimately matter whether one used the rhetoric of disjunction or of continuity, as long as the feel for the immediacy of suffering was maintained and suffering was not reified through an ornate sophisticated intellectual packaging.

The reaffirmation of the language of self could be briefly described as a part of an old dialectic. The modern world view challenges the traditional faith that greater self-realization

---

un-Indian concept of a sinful childhood which could be atoned for in adulthood only through the reparative gesture of public service. See Erikson, *Gandhi's Truth*.

leads to greater understanding of the not-self, including the material world. Modernity includes the faith that the more human beings understand or control the 'objective' not-self, including the not-self in the self (the id, the brain processes, social or biological history), the more they control and understand the self (the ego, praxis, consciousness). A non-modern person, if using Freudian or Marxian categories, would argue the other way round: the more he understands his ego or his praxis, he would say, the more he understands the universal primary processes of the id as well as the universal dialecti. of history. It is possible that the non-modern civilizations had to some extent exhausted the critical or creative possibilities of this primacy given to self-realization when modernity began to stress the other side of the story. But modernity in turn had over-corrected for the staleness of the older vision when critical traditionalists like Thoreau, Tolstoy and Gandhi began to re-emphasize the world views which, through self-control and self-realization, sought to understand and change the world.

It was as a part of these two languages that Gandhi broke out of the determinism of history. His concept of a free India, his solution to racial, caste and inter-religious conflicts and his concept of human dignity were remarkably free from the constraints of history. Whatever their other flaws, they gave societies the option of choosing their futures here and now—without heroes, without high drama and without a constant search for originality, discontinuous changes and final victories. They were the Indian version of historians 'who impose dominion upon fact instead of surrendering to it'.[99] If the past does not bind social consciousness and the future begins here, the present is the 'historical' moment, the permanent yet shifting point of crisis and the time for choice. One can either call it an Oriental version of the concept of permanent revolution or a practical extension of the mystical concept of timeless time in some Asiatic traditions.

With this, Gandhi rounded up his critique of the colonial

[99] Ellmann, 'The Critic as Artist as Wilde', p. 30.

consciousness and proceeded to fight the organized aspects of colonialism. That second battle does not concern us here.

VIII

I started with the proposition that colonialism is first of all a matter of consciousness and needs to be defeated ultimately in the minds of men. In the rest of this essay I have tried to identify two major psychological categories or stratificatory principles derived from biological differences which gave structure to the ideology of colonialism in India under British rule and to show how these principles related the colonial culture to the subject community, and ensured the survival of colonialism in the minds of men. I have also, I hope, shown that the liberation ultimately had to begin from the colonized and end with the colonizers. As Gandhi was to so clearly formulate through his own life, freedom is indivisible, not only in the popular sense that the oppressed of the world are one but also in the unpopular sense that the oppressor too is caught in the culture of oppression.

One question now remains to be answered. In examining parts of the mindscape of British colonialism in India I have gone back into time. Has that time travel observed the rules of history or is it also a matter of a myth? Did Gandhi really construct human nature and society the way I have described? Or is mine a second-order construction—a secondary elaboration, as a psychoanalyst may prefer to call it—which imputes to a man a new structure in the manner of India's traditional commentators on persons and texts? Perhaps the question is irrelevant. As Gandhi so effortlessly demonstrated, for those seeking liberation, history can sometimes be made to follow from myths.

Two

The Uncolonized Mind:
A Post-Colonial View of India
and the West

I

Rudyard Kipling (1862–1936) thought he knew which side of
the great divide between imperial Britain and subject India
he stood. He was certain that to be ruled by Britain was India's
right; to rule India was Britain's duty. He was also certain
that, as one with a knowledge of both their cultures, he had
the responsibility to define both the right and the duty. But
is it the whole story? Or is it the last line of a story which
began years ago, in Kipling's childhood in India?

Angus Wilson begins his biography of Kipling by saying that
Kipling was 'a man who, throughout his life, worshipped and
respected . . . children and their imaginings.'[1] Kipling's early
life provides a clue to the childhood he worshipped and
respected. He was not merely born in India; he was brought
up in India by Indian servants in an Indian environment. He
thought, felt and dreamt in Hindustani, mainly communicated
with Indians, and even looked like an Indian boy.[2] He went to
Hindu temples, for he was 'below the age of caste', and once,
when he visited a farm with his parents, he walked away holding the hand of a farmer, saying to his mother in Hindustani:
'Goodbye, this is my brother.'

Young Kipling was deeply impressed by the romance, the

---

[1] *The Strange Ride of Rudyard Kipling* (New York: Viking, 1977), p. 1.

[2] Edmund Wilson, 'The Kipling that Nobody Read', in Andrew Rutherford
(ed.), *Kipling's Mind and Art: Selected Critical Essays* (Stanford, California: Stanford
University Press, 1964), pp. 17–69. See p. 18.

colour and the mystery of India. And the country became a permanent part of his idea of an idyllic childhood, associated with his 'years of *safe* delight' and his private 'garden of Eden before the fall'.[3] To speak of this memory as the core of his adult self may seem overly psychological, but certainly no other non-Indian writer of English has equalled Kipling's sensitivity to Indian words, to India's flora and fauna, and to the people who inhabit India's 600,000 villages. The Indian peasantry remained for him his beloved children throughout his life.[4]

As against this affinity to things Indian, there was his close-yet-distant relationship with his Victorian parents. He interacted with them mainly when he was formally—and somewhat ritually—presented to them by the servants. When speaking to his parents, his autobiography states, he 'haltingly translated out of the vernacular idiom that one thought and dreamt in.'[5] Overtly, his love, respect and gratitude to his parents, specially his mother, were immense. Yet, at least one biographer has pointed out the gap between 'the elevated, almost religious concept' of a mother's place in a son's life, as found in Kipling's stories and verses, and his own relationship with his mother.[6] Mother Alice Kipling was not apparently a woman who encouraged much emotionalism.

Also, it was through his parents that Rudyard was exposed to the most painful experience of his life. After six idyllic years in Bombay, he was sent with his sister to Southsea in England, to one Aunt Rosa for education and 'upkeep'. Mrs Rosa Holloway belonged to an English family of declining fortunes, and with her husband, a retired army officer, she kept boarders. On the surface everything went smoothly. Some visitors found Mrs Holloway a loving guardian to Rudyard and she did relate well with his sister. But it transpired after Kipling's

---

[3] Edmund Wilson, 'The Kipling that Nobody Read'; Angus Wilson, *The Strange Ride*, p. 3.

[4] Angus Wilson, *The Strange Ride*, p. 4.

[5] *Something of Myself, For My Friends, Known and Unknown* (New York: Doubleday and Doran, 1937), p. 5.

[6] Angus Wilson, *The Strange Ride*, p. 11.

death that his years at Southsea had been a torture. His posthumous autobiography describes Mrs Holloway's establishment as a 'House of Desolation', characterized by restrictions, bullying, persecution and some sadism. The malefactors included both Aunt Rosa and her young son.

It must have been a lonely, hateful world for someone brought up in close proximity to nature, in a free yet capsulating world, peopled by kindly, warm, non-parental figures. To Mrs Holloway, on the other hand, Rudyard was a stranger. Sold to the Victorian and Calvinist concept of a sinful childhood that had to be chastened, she must have found the strong-willed, defiant, uninhibited child particularly spoilt, unsaved and reprobate. Perhaps there was an element of jealousy too. At least one chronicler suggests that both Mrs Holloway and her bully of a son might have sensed that the arrogant deceitful little boy had spent his time in a world quite beyond their dreary horizon.[7]

To young Rudyard, the ill-treatment at Southsea was a great betrayal by his parents. To requote a passage by his sister made famous by Edmund Wilson in the 1940s:

Looking back, I think the real tragedy of our early days, apart from Aunty's bad temper and unkindness to my brother, sprang from our inability to understand why our parents had deserted us. We had had no preparation or explanation; it was like a double death or rather, like an avalanche that had swept away everything happy and familiar . . . We felt that we had been deserted, 'almost as much as on a door-step'. . . . There was no getting out of that, as we often said.[8]

Some have argued that such banishment to England was normal in those times and must be considered well-motivated. Anglo-Indian parents did live with the fear of servants spoiling their children, introducing them to heathenism and encouraging in them sexual precocity. Also, Alice Kipling's third baby had died and she was anxious about her surviving children.

[7] Ibid., p. 32.

[8] 'Some Childhood Memories of Rudyard Kipling', *Chambers Journal*, Eighth Series, VIII (1939), p. 171, quoted in Edmund Wilson, 'The Kipling that Nobody Read', p. 20.

But the issue is not whether Rudyard was justified in feeling what he felt about his parents, but whether he actually harboured such feelings. His sister was the only person to know, and her evidence in this respect is conclusive. The other, and more serious evidence is the fact that he finally had at Southsea a 'severe nervous breakdown', made more horrible by partial blindness and hallucinations.[9]

At last, Rudyard was taken away from Southsea and put in a public school which catered for children of families of a military background, mainly children planning to enter the navy. The school emphasized the military and masculine virtues. Ragging was common, the cultural compulsion to enter sports enormous. But Rudyard was a sedentary, artistically-minded child who hated sports, partly because of his dangerously weak eyesight and partly because he was already sure that he wanted to live a life of the mind. In addition, Kipling looked noticeably a non-white (at least some Indians have observed that Kipling had a tan which could not be explained away as a result of the Indian sun). The result was more misery. If his parents showed him the other side of English affection and Mrs Holloway the other face of English authority, the bullying and ostracism he suffered as an alien-looking 'effeminate' schoolboy gave him another view of the English subculture that produced the ruling élites for the colonies.

In sum, reared in the company of doting Indian servants who desanitized the Victorian though non-Calvinist and non-church-going Kipling family, young Rudyard found England a harrowing experience. It was a culture he could admire—the admiration was also a product of his socialization—but not love. He remained in England a conspicuous bicultural sahib, the English counterpart of the type he was to later despise: the bicultural Indian babu. Others sensed this marginality and the resulting social awkwardness, and this further distanced him from English society in England and subsequently in India. His writings were to reflect this remoteness later, and he never

[9] Edmund Wilson, 'The Kipling that Nobody Read', p. 20.

could write about England as captivatingly as about India.[10]

Yet, his oppressive English years inevitably gave Kipling the message that England was a part of his true self, that he would have to disown his Indianness and learn not to identify with the victims, and that the victimhood he had known in England could be avoided, perhaps even glorified, through identification with the aggressors, especially through loyalty to the aggressors' values.

Kipling himself had been effeminate, weak, individualistic, rebellious and unwilling to see the meaning of life only in work or useful activity (he was bad at figures in his school at Southsea and could not read till he was six). These were exactly the faults he later bitterly attacked in Westernized Indians. Almost self-depreciatingly, he idealized the herd and the pack and the kind of morality which would hold such a collectivity together. He never guessed that it was a short step from the Westernized Indian to the Indianized Westerner and he never realized that the marginality he scorned in the pro-Indian intellectuals and the anti-colonial liberals was actually his own.

What were the links between the two Kiplings: between the hero loyal to Western civilization and the Indianized Westerner who hated the West within him, between the hero who interfaced cultures and the anti-hero who despised cultural hybrids and bemoaned the unclear sense of self in him?

It was blind violence and a hunger for revenge. Kipling was always ready to justify violence as long as it was counterviolence. Edmund Wilson points out, with a touch of contempt, that much of Kipling's work is remarkably free of any real defiance of authority and any sympathy for the victims.[11] Actually there is more to it. Kipling distinguished between the victim who fights well and pays back the tormentor in his own coin and the victim who is passive–aggressive, effeminate, and fights back through non-cooperation, shirking, irresponsibility, malingering and refusal to value face-to-face fights. The first

[10] See on this K. Bhaskara Rao, *Rudyard Kipling's India* (Norman: University of Oklahoma, 1967), pp. 23–4.

[11] Edmund Wilson, 'The Kipling that Nobody Read'.

was the 'ideal victim' Kipling wished to be, the second was the victim's life young Kipling lived and hated living. If he did not have any compassion for the victims of the world, he did not have any compassion for a part of himself either.

But Kipling's literary sensitivities did not entirely fail him even in this sphere. He knew it was not a difference between violence and nonviolence, but between two kinds of violence. The first was the violence that was direct, open and tinged with legitimacy and authority. It was the violence of self-confident cultural groups, used to facing violent situations with overwhelming advantages. The second was the violence of the weak and the dominated, used to facing violence with overwhelming disadvantages. There is in this second violence a touch of non-targeted rage as well as of desperation, fatalism and, as the winners or masters of the world would have it, cowardliness. This violence is often a fantasy rather than an intervention in the real world, a response to the first kind of violence rather than a cause or justification for it.

In Kipling's life, the first kind of violence happened to be the prerogative of the British rulers in India; the second that of Indians subjugated in India. Kipling correctly sensed that the glorification of the victor's violence was the basis of the doctrine of social evolution and ultimately colonialism, that one could not give up the violence without giving up the concept of colonialism as an instrument of progress.

The cost of this moral blindness was enormous. The centre-piece of Kipling's life was a refusal to look within, an aggressive 'anti-intraception' which forced him to avoid all deep conflicts, and prevented him from separating human problems from ethnic stereotypes. Remarkably extraversive, his work stressed all forms of collectivity, and saw the bonds of race and blood as more important than person-to-person relationships. As if their author, he hoped that the restlessness and occasional depression that had dogged him since the Southsea days could be driven off-scent by the extraversive search for cultural roots, through the service he was rendering to the imperial authority. He lived and died fighting his other self—a softer, more creative and happier self—and the uncertainty and self-hatred associated with it.

Simultaneously, the only India he was willing to respect was the one linked to her martial past and subcultures, the India which was a Dionysian counterplayer as well as an ally of the West. Probably, at another plane, like Nirad C. Chaudhuri and V. S. Naipaul after him, Kipling too lived his life searching for an India which, in its hard masculine valour, would be an equal competitor or opponent of the West that had humiliated, disowned and despised his authentic self.

Some critics have spoken of the two voices of Kipling. One, it seems, has even named the voices the saxophone and the oboe. The saxophone was, one suspects, Kipling's martial, violent, self-righteous self which rejected pacifism and glorified soldiery, went through spells of depression, was fascinated by the grotesque and the macabre, and lived with an abiding fear of madness and death. The oboe was Kipling's Indianness and his awe for the culture and the mind of India, his bewilderment at India's heterogeneity and complexity, her incoherence and 'ancient mystery', her resistance to the mechanization of work as well as man, and ultimately her androgyny. The antonyms were masculine hardness and imperial responsibility on the one hand, and feminine softness and cross-cultural empathy, on the other. The saxophone won out, but the oboe continued to play outside Kipling's earshot, trying to keep alive a subjugated strain of his civilization in the perceived weaknesses of another.

II

This long story tells us a number of things about the world of the men who built, ran, or legitimized empires, about the experienced violence which became in them a lifelong fear of and respect for violence, and about the attempt to give meaning to private suffering by developing theories of extraversive violence. This in turn, underneath all the attempts to identify with the aggressor and despite singing the praise of the powerful, was also a matter of 'turning against the self': a defence touching in this case the very margins of self-destructiveness. Such processes provide vital clues to the fates of polities and cultures.

For the moment, however, I shall focus on a dilemma in Kipling's personal life which was common to all colonial ideologies and could be so to most post-colonial awarenesses. This dilemma is important because while the economic, political and moral results of colonialism have been discussed, its emotional and cognitive costs have been ignored. And as Freud has reminded us in this century, what we choose to forget has a tendency to come back to haunt us in 'history'.

Kipling's dilemma can be stated simply: he could not be both Western *and* Indian; he could be either Western *or* Indian. It was this imposed choice which linked his self-destructiveness to the tragedy of his life: Kipling's avowed values were Western, his rejected under-socialized self Indian, and he had to choose between the two. Had it been the other way round, he might have managed as a brown sahib or as a babu at least to acknowledge his bicultural self and reconcile however crudely the East and the West within him.

This apparently trivial, hypothetical difference is the first clue to the way colonialism tried to take over the Western consciousness, to make it congruent with the needs of colonialism, to take away the wholeness of every white man who chose to be a part of the colonial machine, and to give him a new self-definition which, while provincial in its cultural orientation, was universal in its geographical scope.

In retrospect, colonialism did have its triumphs after all. It *did* make Western man definitionally non-Eastern and handed him a self-image and a world view which were basically responses to the needs of colonialism. He could not but be non-Eastern; he could not but be continuously engaged in studying, interpreting and understanding the East as his negative identity.[12] The 'discovery' of the Orient, which Edward Said has so elegantly described,[13] was designed to expel the other Orient

---

[12] The concept of negative identity is of course borrowed from Erik Erikson. See particularly his *Young Man Luther* (New York: Norton, 1958).

[13] Edward Said, *Orientalism* (London: Routledge and Kegan Paul, 1978).

which had once been a part of the medieval European consciousness as an archetype and a potentiality. That other Orient, too, was sometimes seen as an enemy but it was respected, even if grudgingly. It was seen not merely as the habitat of an alternative world view but also as an alternative source of knowledge about the West. Voltaire's China, for example, was not the modern anthropologist's East; it was the humanist's alter ego of the West. The medieval Middle East was the place where many Europeans went to study Aristotle. And even among the first generation of colonialists in British India—among those who were actually the greatest empire builders—there were those like Warren Hastings who felt that they had more to learn from the civilization they ruled than they had to teach.

This other Orient, the Orient which was the Occident's double, did not fit the needs of colonialism; it carried intimations of an alternative, cosmopolitan, multicultural living which was, to change the context of Angus Wilson's expression, beyond the dreary middle-class horizons of Kipling and his English contemporaries. They forced themselves and every bicultural Westerner to make his choice.

On the other side, colonialism tried to supplant the Indian consciousness to erect an Indian self-image which, in its opposition to the West, would remain in essence a Western construction. If the colonial experience made the mainstream Western consciousness definitionally non-Oriental and redefined the West's self-image as the antithesis or negation of the East, it sought to do the reverse with the self-image of the Orient and with the culture of India. Colonialism replaced the normal ethnocentric stereotype of the inscrutable Oriental by the pathological stereotype of the strange, primal but predictable Oriental—religious but superstitious, clever but devious, chaotically violent but effeminately cowardly. Simultaneously, colonialism created a domain of discourse where the standard mode of transgressing such stereotypes was to reverse them: superstitious but spiritual, uneducated but wise, womanly but pacific, and so on and so forth. No colonialism could be complete unless it 'universalized' and enriched its ethnic stereotypes by appropriating the language of defiance of its victims. That was why the cry of the victims of colonialism was ultimately the cry to be heard in another language—unknown to the colonizer and to the anti-colonial movements that he had bred and then domesticated. That is why the rest of this analysis has to seek to understand the colonial legacy in post-colonial India in a language which, while it incorporates the language of the modern world, also tries to remain outside it. The shifts from the past to the present tense in the following pages, and from the present to the past, is a part of the same effort.

India is not non-West; it is India. Outside the small section of Indians who were once exposed to the full thrust of colonialism and are now heirs to the colonial memory, the ordinary Indian has no reason to see himself as a counterplayer or an antithesis of the Western man. The imposed burden to be perfectly non-Western only constricts his, the everyday Indian's, cultural self, just as the older burden of being perfectly Western once narrowed—and still sometimes narrows—his choices in the matter of his and his society's future. The new responsibility forces him to stress only those parts of his culture which are recessive in the West and to underplay both those which his culture shares with the West and those which remain undefined by the West. The pressure to be the obverse of the West distorts the traditional priorities in the Indian's total view of man and universe and destroys his culture's unique *gestalt*. It in fact binds him even more irrevocably to the West.[14]

In this respect, there is a perfect fit here between many versions of Indian nationalism and the world view of the Kiplings. Both share what the Mādhyamika might call the tendency to absolutize the relative differences between cultures.[15] Both seek to set up the East and the West as permanent and natural

---

[14] I need hardly draw attention to the logical and moral sleight-of-hand which helps equate the refusal to be non-West with being Western.

[15] K. Venkata Ramanan, *Nāgārjuna's Philosophy, As Presented in the Mahā-Prajñāpāramitā Śāstra* (Delhi: Motilal Banarsidass, 1978).

antipodes. Both trace their roots to the cultural arrogance of post-Enlightenment Europe which sought to define not only the 'true' West but also the 'true' East. And both have produced social critics who share the naive belief that the resulting cultural poverty has hurt the East more than the West.

Yet, if there is another India, there is also another West. If the former has been the forgotten majority, the latter has been, even more tragically for the globe, the forgotten minority. If the former has been the never-fully-defeated East, the latter has been, at least in this century, the fully subjugated West. That West survives as an esoterica in the West and perhaps, just perhaps, as a living reality at the corners of the non-West. 'Indians are the only surviving Englishmen', Malcolm Muggeridge once reportedly said, in equal exasperation and derision. It can read as an unwitting recognition that the Indian society has held in trusteeship aspects of the West which are lost to the West itself.

Let us, however, for the moment, shelve the problem of the West and concentrate on the Indian predicament and on that other India which is neither pre-modern nor anti-modern but only non-modern. It is the India which has survived the Western onslaught. It coexists with the India of the modernists, whose attempts to identify with the colonial aggressors has produced the pathetic copies of the Western man in the subcontinent, but it rejects most versions of Indian nationalism as bound irrevocably to the West—in reaction, jealousy, hatred, fear and counterphobia. That other India lives as if it recognized that, culturally, it is a choice neither between the East and the West nor between the North and the South. It is a choice—and a battle—between the Apollonian and the Dionysian *within* India and *within* the West.[16] As this century with its developed ability to translate utopias into reality has shown, if such a distinction does not exist in an oppressive culture, it has to be presumed to exist by its victims for maintaining their

---

[16] I was brought up as a social scientist and only recently have found that these two terms have many meanings. I have in mind only the meanings given to them by Ruth Benedict in *Patterns of Culture* (Boston: Houghton Mifflin, 1934).

own sanity and humanness. Thomas Mann, I am told, affirmed after the Nazi experience that there were not two Germanies but one. Perhaps it is for the Manns to own up the singleness of Germany. For the victims of Germany, at some plane there have to be but two Germanies interlinked if necessary by a single cognitive and ethical discourse.

In the modern West, this battle between the Apollonian and the Dionysian has only marginally involved the East—whether it should have involved the East or not is an altogether different issue. In the East the battle *has* involved the West. Mainstream Indian culture does implicitly recognize that, in terms of the themes central to it, it is not a matter of adjusting to or fighting the might and the world view of the West as an outside agency. Because while the West, in spite of all its theories of martial races and ignoble and noble savages, does not probably incorporate India, India does incorporate the West. T. K. Mahadevan quotes an odd statement of Gandhi which dramatizes this predicament:

Everyone of the Indians who has achieved anything worth mentioning in any direction is the fruit, directly or indirectly, of western education. At the same time, whatever reaction for the better he may have had upon the people at large was due to the extent of his eastern culture.[17]

The absolute rejection of the West is also the rejection of the basic configuration of the Indian traditions; though, paradoxically, the acceptance of that configuration may involve a qualified rejection of the West.

This is the underside of non-modern India's ethnic universalism. It is a universalism which takes into account the colonial experience, including the immense suffering colonialism brought, and builds out of it a maturer, more contemporary, more self-critical version of Indian traditions. It is a universalism which sees the Westernized India as a subtradition which, in spite of its pathology and its tragi-comic core, is a 'digested' form of another civilization that had once gate-

[17] T. K. Mahadevan, *Dvija* (New Delhi: Affiliated East-West Press, 1977), pp. 118–19.

crashed into India. India *has* tried to capture the differentia of the West within its own cultural domain, not merely on the basis of a view of the West as politically intrusive or as culturally inferior, but as a subculture meaningful in itself and important, though not all-important, in the Indian context. This is what I meant when I said that Kipling, when he wanted to be Western, could not be both Western and Indian, whereas the everyday Indian, even when he remains only Indian, is both Indian and Western.

If the East and the West never seem to meet in India, as both Kipling and E. M. Forster seem to argue, it is because of this internality of the West at different levels and areas of Indian life.[18] Familiarity can breed distance, too. If most of the society is spared the problem of handling the West at the deepest levels of consciousness, if there exists a prior endogenous West or a West with its own limited place in Indian cosmology, there is no reason why the Westerner should be seen as a total intruder or, for that matter, as the all-important intruder. Nor is there any reason why the cultural conflict between the East and the West should be seen as the central conflict in Indian life. True, in the process the exposed sections of Indian society have been left to themselves to work through their fears of liminality and rootlessness—'awkwardly suspended between two worlds', as V. G. Kiernan puts it. It is also true that the low concern with the East–West issue in large parts of the society has left these exposed sections doubly concerned with the differences between the Indian and the non-Indian, and the 'us' and the 'they' and forced them to fight a running battle with their feelings of self-hatred and powerlessness. But even the exposed Indians, with nearly four hundred years of exposure to the West, have not been fully deprived of their self-confidence *vis-à-vis* the West; even they carry the intimations of an inner conviction that they would not be swept off their

[18] E. M. Forster in *A Passage to India* (London: Arnold, 1967) ventures the colonial culture as an explanation of this separation and in that form it is an attenuated version of the argument of Frantz Fanon in *The Wretched of the Earth*, trans. Constance Farrington (Harmondsworth: Penguin, 1967).

feet and that they could use the Occident for their own purposes. Even the crafty babus, as Kipling recognized in utter
disgust, know how to use the white man; they too have a theory
of the West.

Only recently have we caught up with the full implications
of this. I find J. Duncan M. Derrett saying in 1979:

It was supposed, and the author of this paper used to suppose along
with his elders and betters, that Indians had learnt English ways and
values as they had learnt the English language, and that, as a race of
would-be parrots they 'have done remarkably well....' One perceived with pained surprise the conflict between profession and performance. Indians trained almost exclusively in Western arts and
sciences reacted as irredeemable orientals in any crisis. They re-
inforced this feeling again and again by their lack of confidence when
faced with a new problem, their pathetic desire for foreign advice
(which they would shelve when they had paid for it), and their 'going
through the motions' like a tight-rope walker who walks his rope for
the sake of walking it, or like a somnambulist, avoiding desperate
accidents but unable to say why.... Very late in the day the present
writer woke up to what he believes to be the fact, namely that Indian
tradition has been 'in charge' throughout, and that English ideas and
English ways, like the English language, have been used for Indian
purposes. That, in fact, it is the British who were manipulated, the
British who were the silly somnambulists. My Indian brother is not a
brown Englishman, he is an Indian who has learned to move around
in my drawing room, and will move around in it so long as it suits
him for his own purposes. And when he adopts my ideas he does so to
suit himself, and retains them so far and as long as it suits him.[19]

Derrett could have added, 'In right understanding (*dharmāṇām
bhūtapratyavekṣā*) not only is revealed the determinate as determinate but there is also in it the indeterminate or the uncondi-
tioned.'[20] Like all devious Orientals, the Indians, even when
they seem totally controlled, do retain some indeterminateness
and freedom. It is another matter that the carriers of the
tradition of the babus, the lowest of the low among the brown
sahibs, whom Kipling so obviously hated, could never take

[19] 'Tradition and Law in India', in R. J. Moore (ed.), *Tradition and Politics in
South Asia* (New Delhi: Vikas, 1979), pp. 32–59. See especially pp. 34–5.
[20] Venkata Ramanan, *Nāgārjuna's Philosophy*, p. 39.

pride in the fact that while they could dare to be part-Kiplings, Kipling could never dare to be a part-babu.

What about the subcategory called the martial Indian, 'the one who was Kipling's truest Indian? And what about Kipling's authentic imperial ruler, the over-burdened white man, with his civilizing mission and his fear that, unless careful, he would regress into the savagery of the people he was ordained to rule? Were there native constructions of them, too, or were they merely seen as strange, archetypal anti-gods who had become a part of one's fate? Evidently, there does exist within the living traditions of India the Dionysian aspect of the modern West as an identifiably Indian subtradition, as the demonic self or *asura prakṛti*:

> *Idamadya mayā labdhamidam prāpsye manoratham,*
> *Idamastīdamapi me bhaviṣyati punardhanam.*
> *Asau mayā hatah śatruh haniṣye cāparānapi,*
> *Īśvaro'hamaham bhogī siddho'ham balavān sukhī*
> *Ādhyo'bhijanavānasmi ko'nyo'sti sadṛśo mayā.*[21]

Asuratva may be generally a negation of virtues in Indian society, but it can be seen sometimes as the pathology of Kṣatriyahood. It is a Kṣatriyahood which has run amuck.[22] Probably this is the framework within which Kipling's imperial consciousness—including the British construction of the native ideology of the martial races—was fitted. Kipling, provincial more by choice than by circumstance, thought that the ideology of Kṣatriyahood was true Indianness, apart from being consistent with the world view of colonialism. He missed the limited role given to Kṣatriyahood in traditional Indian cosmology and

---

[21] 'I wanted this, and today I got it. I want that: I shall get it tomorrow. All these riches are now mine: soon I shall have more. I have killed this enemy. I will kill all the rest. I am ruler of men. I enjoy the things of this world. I am successful, strong and happy. I am so wealthy and so nobly born. Who is my equal?' *Gītā*, Chapter 16, Ślokas 13–15. The translation follows *Bhagavad-Gītā*, trans. Swami Prabhavananda and Christopher Isherwood (Madras: Sri Ramakrishna Math, 1974), p. 240.

[22] Richard Lannoy seems to recognize a part of the dynamic in his *The Speaking Tree: A Study of Indian Culture and Society* (London: Oxford University Press, 1975), p. 256, when he says 'From the viewpoint of the traditional society, Westernization is an extension of Kshatryaization.'

the vested interest his kind had in denying these limits in a colonial culture organized around violence and counter-violence, manhood and maximized potency, and a theory of history that saw all civilizations in terms of the high and the low and the justifiably powerful and the deservedly weak. It is the different weightages given to the martial and the non-martial in the Indian culture that Kipling knew but required to forget.

III

Consistent naturalism or humanism is distinct from both idealism and materialism, and constitutes at the same time the unifying truth of both. . . . Only naturalism is capable of comprehending the action of world history.

Karl Marx[23]

I have argued that the Kiplings sought to redefine, on behalf of the modern West, the Indian as the antonym of the Western man and the Western man as a legitimate conqueror and a ruler. I have also argued that unlike in the West, these new definitions were not deeply internalized by most Indians who already had their native analogues of the modern Western man. They saw the Western man as a transient ruler who like all transient rulers tended to live with illusions of permanence. However, the imperial consciousness did manage to take over some parts of Westernized Indian consciousness. I shall now briefly tell one part of that story, using as my example the way the experience of colonialism has forced the Westernized Indian to first split the Indian self-image and then reconstitute it by showing one part of the image to be false.

India has 'always been a separate world, hard for any outsider, *Eastern or Western*, to penetrate.'[24] Such a culture becomes a projective test; it invites one not only to project on to it one's deepest fantasies, but also to reveal, through such self-projec-

[23] *Economic and Philosophic Manuscripts of 1844* (Moscow: Progress Publishers, 1974), p. 135.

[24] V. G. Kiernan, *The Lords of Human Kind: European Attitudes to the Outside World in the Imperial Age* (Harmondsworth: Penguin, 1972), p. 71. Emphasis added.

tion, the interpreter rather than the interpreted All interpretations of India are ultimately autobiographical. Predictably, a
subgroup of Kipling's Indian brain-children have set up the
martial India as the genuine India which would one day defeat
the West at its own game. They wait for that glorious day and
are quite willing to alter the whole of Indian culture to bring
that victory a little closer, like the American army officer in
Vietnam who once destroyed a village to save it from its
enemies. They demystify the ordinary Indian as a pseudo-
alternative to the Western man: hypocritically spiritual while
being shrewdly materialistic, violent and self-interested; neither
a dedicated counterplayer of the West like Japan, trying to
defeat the West at its own game, nor clearly Oriental like
Confucian China, which, while manifestly hostile to the West,
shares with the West some basic values like performance,
organization and instrumental rationality; neither a person
who meets the norm of civility in the West, nor openly a noble
savage. The cultural ideal of these new Kṣatriyas is a hard
Indian state backed by tough this-worldliness.

In reaction, others have identified the spiritual India as the
real India. To them, therefore, all deviance from spiritualism is
a deviance from Indianness itself. As against the materialism of
the modern West, they see India providing an axis for a dis-
senting global consciousness. The West, according to this view,
is already defeated by the superior Eastern civilizations; it only
obstinately refuses to admit the fact.

Is the perception of such contradictions undetermined by
culture? Must a society always choose between materialism
and spiritualism, between hard realities and unreal dreams?
Or is the perception of such a choice itself a product of Kipling's imperial mission?

True to the description of ethnocentrism in some contemporary studies of the authoritarian personality, the British colonial attitude to Indian culture was always inconsistent. On
the one hand the British saw the Indian as overly this-worldly—
exceedingly shrewd, greedy, self-centred, money-minded. On
the other hand, they also despised the Indian as overly other-

worldly—not fit for the world of modern science and tech-, nology, statecraft and productive work. (The colonizer in India thus proved, if such a proof was necessary, that an oppressive system seeks legitimation in all available ways. Spiritualism in British India was never the only opiate.) This is a split which has persisted in India's modern sector. Once other explanations of India's problems are exhausted, the modern Indian is always tempted to fall back upon either the stereotype of the spiritual Indian or on that of the pseudo-spiritual.

It is doubtful if most Indians look at India this way. India is not merely its spiritual self. The society *does* give an important place to spirituality, but it is hardly the overwhelming aspect of Indianness. The plethora of empirical studies done from Marxist as well as structural–functional vantage grounds should have at least made us aware that underlying much Indian spirituality lie this-worldly choices, hard self-interest, and reality-testing. This however has not stopped anyone, not even the scholars who have done these studies, from exhorting the Indians to be more this-worldly and more realistic. Even a scholar as erudite as D. D. Kosambi has a touch of innocence about him when he accuses the Gītā in the same paragraph of 'slippery opportunism' and of admitting that 'material reality is a gross illusion'.[25] Similarly with Indian materialism. After all the materialist interpretations are exhausted, there remains an irreducible element of spiritual concerns which informs the toughest materialism in India. Sometimes this element is seen as the residual irrationality of a person whose flesh is willing but whose heart is weak—a reversal of metaphor which has its own story to tell. Sometimes it is seen as simple hypocrisy, a political compromise with the superstitious Indian masses who have more power than acumen. But the fact remains that from rationalist social critic Rammohun Roy's (1772–1833) prayerful last days at Bristol to agnostic Jawaharlal Nehru's (1889–1964) mystical last will and testament it is the same story of time travel through the *āśramas* of life.

Perhaps only in a Cartesian consciousness does the India of

[25] D. D. Kosambi, *Myth and Reality* (Bombay: Popular Prakashan, 1962), p. 17.

Ananda Coomaraswamy and Sarvepalli Radhakrishnan negate the India of D. D. Kosambi and Devi Prasad Chattopadhyaya, only within the modern awareness do the two Indias become two ideologies competing for the minds of men, instead of being two strains within the same life style, dialectically inter-related and complementary.[26] This is another way of saying that the two Indias which the ideologies project are both pro-ducts of Western intrusion and both are attempts to reconstruct Indian culture according to categories which would seem internally consistent to the modern Western mind. Both are attempts to convert levels of living—or aspects of selfhood—into types of ideology.

In the Indian world view, as in most world views once we have unlearnt to see them as objects of professional study, even the most recalcitrant of ideologies can be read as a level or phase of living or as a response to a specific ontological or existential problem. A plurality of ideologies can always be accommodated within a single life style. Fittingly so; a living culture has to live and it has an obligation to itself, not to its analysts. Even less does it have any obligation to conform to a model, its own or someone else's. Modern scholars of course have their own obligation to their disciplines; they cannot afford to grant the convertibility between life styles and ideo-logies. They have to reconcile the self-created 'contradiction' between the materialist and the idealist India by unmasking one of the Indias as false.

Thus one is caught in a peculiar dilemma in modern India.

[26] Actually the point can be made neatly through a comparison of the works of, say, Radhakrishnan and Chattopadhyaya. In a strange way the two views can become each other's captive opposites. See particularly S. Radhakrishnan, *Indian Philosophy* (Bombay: Blackie, 1977), vol. 1; and *The Hindu View of Life* (London, 1926); D. P. Chattopadhyaya, *Lokāyata: A Study in Ancient Indian Materialism* (New Delhi: People's Publishing House, 1973); and *What is Living and What is Dead in Indian Philosophy* (New Delhi: People's Publishing House, 1977). Alan Roland in his forthcoming, as-yet-untitled work on the Indian personality treats this com-plementarity in terms of a tripartite division of the self into the spiritual, the familial and the individuated. There is here an isomorphism between the cultural and the psychological.

On the one side, there are the modern cult figures who stress the spiritual India to exclude the materialist India from India. As they themselves become commodities in the Western market-place of spiritualism and instant salvation, as they become more and more dependent on major structures of the modern world, as they legitimize ancient thought through modern science, and as they adapt traditional knowledge for solving modern prob-lems at the risk of trivializing both, these gurus reportedly rediscover for the Indians their true spiritual destiny!

On the other side are those who 'see through' Indian spiri-tualism and find underneath only second-class materialism. Only by debunking the spiritual India can the Nirad C. Chaudhuris and the V. S. Naipauls become the counterpoints to the modern *maharṣis* and *ācāryas*.[27] Only as professional debunkers are they a part of the modern world of the pro-fessional godmen. Like the godmen they reject, they also use the modern world to propagate their versions of India. Only instead of selling the spiritual India and explaining away the materialist, they vend the materialist India and debunk the spiritual. Being inverted modern gurus, they cannot forgive India for not being either a true copy or a true counterplayer of the West. They hate the confused self-definition of the Indian more than what they see as the society's major failures. The Hindu, for instance, is aggressive while talking of pacifism, dirty in spite of his ideology of purity, materialist while preach-ing spiritualism, and comically Indian when trying to be Western.[28]

Persons can be hypocrites. Can cultures also be so? Does the hypocrisy of cultures on closer scrutiny turn out to be a con-tradiction in the human condition itself? For that matter, is a hypocrite only a casual cheat? Or is he someone who reaffirms the basic human values in a world hostile to such values, while

---

[27] Nirad C. Chaudhuri, *The Continent of Circe* (London: Chatto and Windus, 1965); V. S. Naipaul, *An Area of Darkness* (London: André Deutsch, 1964) and *India: A Wounded Civilization* (London: André Deutsch, 1977).

[28] See particularly Chaudhuri, *The Continent of Circe*, Chapter 5.

himself succumbing to worldly temptations? Is a hypocrite an unwilling critic of everyday life whose personal failure signals a larger cultural crisis?

Probably the answers are less complex than the questions. India after all is not outside the world. Certainly, for centuries, it has mounted the same chaotic, part-sincere search for a humane society that other parts of the world have mounted. Certainly, many of India's experiments in civilized social life, too, have been makeshift efforts to survive enormous odds. Many of these experiments have failed and many of the culture's dreams, too, have turned into nightmares.

In addition, in recent centuries, the society has had to make major compromises with outer forces of oppression, backed by the powerful ideology of modernity and by an all-conquering technology, and it is still struggling to work through that experience. It has been forced to cultivate the creative self-protection which the victims often show when faced with an inescapable situation: a slightly comical imitativeness which indirectly reveals the ridiculousness of the powerful; an instrumental use of the ways of the powerful, which overtly grants their superiority yet denies their culture (this may involve the rejection of values such as work, productivity, masculinity, maturity or adulthood, rationality and normality); an uncanny ability to subvert the valued skills or traits which may ensure one's adaptation to the 'system' (such as intelligence, creativity, achievement, adjustment, personal growth or development); an over-done obsequiousness which indirectly seeks to limit the options of the target of ingratiation; and a stylized other-worldliness which can disarm at least those who see it as a denial of self-interest.

The pathology of the Westernized Indian's personality, which Kipling so cleverly identified, was rooted in India's encounter with the ego-ideals of Kipling in the first place. The Chaudhuris and the Naipauls are not only critics of an inevitable mode of self-defence, they are also a part of it. They provide 'secondary elaborations' of a culture designed to hide

the real self—the deepest social consciousness of the victims—
from the outsiders.

The determinate is not that determined after all.

IV

Probably in such a world, once the codes of both Indian
materialism and Indian spiritualism are cracked, both can be
shown to share the same or complementary concerns. Let me
examine this mutuality in the life of Sri Aurobindo (1872–
1950), who in many ways was a counterpoint to Kipling. I hope
to show that between Kipling and Aurobindo, the latter's
response to colonialism included a cultural self-affirmation
which had a greater respect for the selfhood of the 'other' and a
search for a more universal model of emancipation, however
sick or bizarre that search may seem to many of us. In fact, it
could be argued that the 'sickness' or the 'bizarreness' was
itself a product of the colonial culture, telescoped deep into the
personal life of Aurobindo. Aurobindo's spiritualism can be
seen as a way of handling a situation of cultural aggression and
to that extent it was a language of defiance, seeking to make
sense out of the West in Indian terms. It is a matter of judge-
ment how far the attempt made sense to his society and how
far it remained a *reductio* of the West's version of the other-
worldly Indian.

Kipling was culturally an Indian child who grew up to
become an ideologue of the moral and political superiority of
the West. Aurobindo was culturally a European child who
grew up to become a votary of the spiritual leadership of India.
Kipling had to disown his Indianness to become his concept of
the true European; Aurobindo had to own up his Indianness to
become his version of the authentic Indian. However, while
both could be seen as products of the psychopathology of
colonialism, Aurobindo symbolized a more universal response
to the splits which colonialism induced. He, after all, did not
have to disown the West within him to become his version of

an Indian. To the end of his life Western culture remained a
vehicle of his creative self-expression and he never thought the
West to be outside the reach of God's grace. Even when he
spoke of race and evolution, two of the most dangerous themes
in Western cosmology, not once did he use the concepts to
divide humankind; he always had the human race and human
evolution in mind. And during the Second World War, when he
made the stunning claim that his yoga was determining the
course of the war in Europe and deciding the fate of Japan, he
knew on which side in the climactic battles he wanted to be
and which strain in which civilization he wanted to save
through his psychic powers. Nazi Germany to him always remained a satanic force and, though the rebirth of Asia was one
of his fondest dreams, he abhorred Japanese militarism to the
end.[29] One is forced to conclude that, compared to Kipling's
'sickness of soul', Aurobindo's sickness of mind was a superior
cognition of the human predicament and it did show, long
before the R. D. Laings entered the scene, that even the
deepest feelings of grandeur and depersonalization could carry
intimations of an alternative political morality.

The point can be made in another way. While Aurobindo
belonged to the tradition of the most deeply reactive of the
Indian responses to colonialism—the one which partly drew
inspiration from Bankimchandra and Vivekananda—he always
had, like Bankimchandra and Vivekananda, a genuine place
for the West within Indian civilization. For Kipling on the
other hand, India was not a civilization which enjoyed equal
rights; it was a geographical area one could love and a socio-

---

[29] This was particularly noteworthy for two reasons. First, many of his ac-
quaintances from his earlier political days, as well as younger political leaders like
Subhas Chandra Bose whom he so admired, were seeking the help of Germany
and Japan to oust the British from India. Many of these young leaders had been
deeply influenced by Aurobindo's earlier political ideology and record. Second,
he was perfectly aware of the possibility of misuse by the Allies of their victory in
the war. On his yogic intervention in the war, see Sri Aurobindo, *On Himself*
(Pondicherry: Sri Aurobindo Ashram, 1972), pp. 38–9, 393–9; see also p. 388 for
his comments on Lenin and the Russian Revolution which seem to suggest that
Aurobindo himself did not think of his yogic interventions in the 'world forces' in
too concretistic terms.

logical space where you, if you were a real 'man', could find yourself. This certainly was not accidental. Aurobindo was above all a victim who had fashioned out of his victimhood a new meaning for suffering and a new model of defiance. As a victim, he protected—and had to protect—his humanity and moral sanity more carefully because, while the colonial system only saw him as an object, he could not see the colonizers as mere objects. As a part of his struggle for survival, the West remained for Indian victims like Aurobindo an internal human reality, in love as well as in hate, in identification as well as in counter-identification.

Aurobindo Ackroyd Ghose—the Western middle name was given by his father at birth—was the third son of his parents. The Ghoses were urbane Brahmos from near Calcutta and fully exposed to the new currents of social change in India. Father Krishnadhan, a doctor trained in England, was in government service. He was well known among his friends and relatives for his aggressively Anglicized ways. He forbade his children to learn or speak Bengali; even at home they had to converse in English. Their dress and food, too, were English. In addition, Krishnadhan was an atheist and he tried hard to protect his children from the ill-effects of Hinduism. For some reason, young Aurobindo was the favoured object of his father's zealous social engineering. Krishnadhan 'took the greatest care that nothing Indian should touch this son of his.'[30]

Mother Swarnalata, about whom 'official' biographers seem reticent, was the daughter of Raj Narayan Bose, the renowned scholar, religious leader, social reformer and nationalist. She herself was known mainly for her beauty. Though coming from a reformist family and married to a highly Westernized man, Swarnalata was an orthodox Hindu, and it is almost certain that she did not fully relish the Western manners of her husband. Nor must she have enjoyed the charade of com-

---

[30] Sisirkumar Mitra, *The Liberator: Sri Aurobindo, India and the World* (Delhi: Jaico, 1954), p. 24. Also Satprem, *Sri Aurobindo or The Adventure of Consciousness*, trans. Tehmi (Pondicherry: Sri Aurobindo Ashram, 1968), Chapter 1.

municating through English in the family. However, what disturbed human relations in the family more than the oppression of language was the illness Swarnalata fell prey to early in Aurobindo's life. Called hysteria by her contemporaries, it was obviously the early stage of something more serious. Though her father took her to his house at Deoghar to convalesce, she gradually became more and more 'unmanageable'. Meanwhile Krishnadhan installed a mistress at home.

Time has erased the details of Swarnalata's illness; we merely know that her side of the family had a number of 'hysterics' and that her illness was associated with occasional bouts of violence towards her children. (There was at least one instance when young Aurobindo stood, stupefied and fearful, witnessing his mother beating his elder brother.[31]) We also know that either as a response to her or as a general response to the environment at home, young Aurobindo showed signs of mutism and interpersonal withdrawal, which his admirers were to later read as an early sign of spirituality.[32]

The West continued to oppress Aurobindo in other ways, too. When five, he was sent to a totally Westernized, élite convent at Darjeeling with an English governess who served as a surrogate mother. His co-students there were mostly white. English was the sole medium of instruction and the only means of communication outside school hours. The resulting sense of exile found expression, even at that age, in a statement made in the third person: 'In the shadow of the Himalayas, in sight of the wonderful snow-capped peaks, even in their native land they were brought up in alien surroundings.'[33] When he had his first paranormal experience at Darjeeling, it carried the impress of this loneliness and depression. He had the vision of a heavy,

---

[31] Niradbaran, *Sri Aurobindāyan* (Calcutta: Sri Aurobindo Pathmandir, 1980), 3rd ed., p. 17.

[32] Only one of them slips into the shrewd observation in his hagiography that Aurobindo never cared much about any of his relatives except his maternal grandfather. Pramodkumar Sen, *Sri Aurobindo: Jīvan o Yog* (Calcutta: Sri Aurobindo Pathmandir, 1977), pp. 9–10.

[33] Aurobindo quoted in K. R. Srinivasa Iyengar, *Sri Aurobindo* (Calcutta: Arya Publishing House, 1950), p. 15.

palpable darkness speedily descending on to earth and entering him. The darkness stayed with him for the next fourteen years.

Aurobindo was seven when his parents took him and two of his brothers to England and left them there. They were now to be exposed, not to the Westernized life style of Indians but to the Western ways of the English. At London, the brothers were put under the tutelage of an English couple, the Reverend and Mrs Drewett, who were given 'strict instructions' not to allow the children 'to make the acquaintance of any Indian or undergo any Indian influence. These instructions were carried out to the letter.'[34] The Drewetts were also told by Krishnadhan to spare his sons all religious education. (The Reverend Drewett's mother, however, being more consistent in her Christian evangelism, worried about Aurobindo's soul. One Sunday she did manage to get him duly baptized as a Christian.)

During his days with the Drewetts and later at an élite school at London, Aurobindo was exposed to the classical heritage of Europe, especially to Latin and Greek. He also began to write and publish poetry in Latin, Greek and English.[35] Afterwards he took a scholarship to King's College, Cambridge, where, too, he did brilliantly in the classics, winning all the relevant prizes for one year. He also dutifully learnt French, some German and Italian. There was still no rebellion in the air.

Scholarly success however was no protection against the deep economic and nurtural anxieties to which Aurobindo and his brothers were sometimes subjected in England. Their father, though wealthy, stopped sending them money for no clear reason. And the three brothers lived in acute poverty. Added to this was Aurobindo's loneliness; he had no close relationship with anyone in England.[36] The result was an 'inward depression' which in middle age Aurobindo was once to mention

---

[34] Mitra, *The Liberator*, p. 25.

[35] The interest in poetry was to persist and Aurobindo's most creative work was to remain an English epic, *Savitri*, which he began writing in his twenties and completed shortly before his death. Aurobindo considered himself a poet first. Niradbaran, *Sri Aurobindāyan*, p. 40.

[36] Aurobindo, *On Himself*, p. 7. Also Aurobindo's letter to Dilip (1935) quoted in Srinivasa Iyengar, *Sri Aurobindo*, p. 19.

casually.[37] The other result was more predictable. For years he had been taught to view England as an ideal society; now England was re-invoking his early anxieties associated with the West.

At last Aurobindo began to look for alternative ways of handling the Occident and to defy the model of success associated with the Anglicism of his father.[38] Thus, after taking the first part of the Classical Tripos with a first class, Aurobindo did not take the degree. And worse, though he did very well in the Indian Civil Service examination, he missed the riding test and got himself disqualified, knowing fully that 'his father was very particular' about the examination.[39] Finally, Aurobindo delivered a few fiery nationalist speeches at the Indian Majlis in Cambridge and got involved with an incipient secret society pursuing the cause of Indian freedom.

As if to symbolize his break with the West, Aurobindo dropped the Ackroyd from his name during this period of his stay in England.

After fourteen years in England and after thorough denationalization—the expression was his—Aurobindo came back to India. He found his father dead; he had died heart-broken on hearing the rumour that the ship carrying Aurobindo home had sunk. And Aurobindo was soon to find out that his mother, now in an advanced stage of insanity, could recognize him only with difficulty. However, by this time he was already moving towards new parental figures. Already, on touching the soil of India, the darkness that had haunted him since his Darjeeling days had lifted and he had had the experience of being enveloped by a deep calm and silence.[40] After all, he had come back

---

[37] Aurobindo, *On Himself*, p. 20.

[38] He was helped in this by the traditions of the mother's side of his family—Raj Narayan Bose anticipated some of the tenets of Hindu nationalism—and by his unpredictable father's other self. Krishnadhan might have faltered on their allowance, but he did not fail to send his sons in England a nationalist periodical published from Calcutta, with its accounts of British oppression in India underlined.

[39] Mitra, *The Liberator*, p. 26.   [40] Ibid., p. 34.

to his motherland, to learn his mother tongue and, as we shall soon find out, to discover the primal authority of the mother.

Aurobindo started his life in Baroda as a bureaucrat and a language teacher. He had learnt some Bengali and Sanskrit in England from an *English* scholar; he brushed these up in Baroda and also picked up Marathi and Gujarati. He had been always good at languages and public speaking; now, as he turned quieter in personal life, he became more expressive in his formal communication. He began to write for nationalist journals and gradually became a major public figure. It was at Baroda again that he first found out his spiritual powers. Once he saved himself from an accident when a divine, luminous self separated itself from his own body and took control of his horse-drawn carriage; another time he saw a living presence in an icon of Kālī.

In 1901, Aurobindo got married. His bride Mrinalini Devi was, to go by her father's account, an attractive but otherwise ordinary girl of fourteen. She was made to pay for her ordinariness. Though Aurobindo chose her himself, he was soon to lose interest in her—when it became clear that she would be unable to live up to his expectations. Mrinalini died childless, lonely, heart-broken and perhaps unlamented in 1918, some years after Aurobindo renounced the world. By that time, she had suffered from Aurobindo's long absences from home and from expectations that he would come back and take her into his new life. Till the end, she was innocently to try to become acceptable to him through her religious activities, relying on his vague hints that he might return to her.[41] He never did. The pathetic essay which her father wrote after her death, though doctored by the Aurobindo Ashram, brings out the tragedy of a simple, doting wife, crushed by forces of which she had no comprehension.

Neither his spiritual quest nor his marriage stopped Aurobindo from being drawn into the vortex of the national st

[41] Part of an untitled essay by Mrinalini's father published in *Sri Aurobinder Patra, Mrinalinike Likhita* (Pondicherry: Sri Aurobindo Ashram, 1977), first expanded edition, pp. 31–5; see p. 33.

movement and he soon became an important leader of the groups fighting for the violent overthrow of British rule. He also became the editor of an important nationalist periodical and the principal of a nationalist college in Calcutta. Simultaneously, he worked out the rudiments of a political ideology. It was built around a vague form of populism in which 'the proletariat' was 'the real key to the situation'[42] and around a mythography of India as a powerful mother, Śakti, who was being oppressed by the West and had to be liberated through blood sacrifices made by her children.

I know my country as Mother. I offer her my devotions, my worship. If a monster sits upon her breast and prepares to suck her blood, what does her child do? Does he quietly sit down to his meal . . . or rush to her rescue? I know I have in me the power to accomplish the deliverance of my fallen country. . . . It is the power of knowledge, *Brahmatej* founded in *Jnana*. This feeling is not new to me . . . with this feeling I was born . . . God has sent me to earth to do this work. . . .[43]

The imagery was of course partly borrowed from Bankimchandra Chatterji, the first to introduce the theme of the great mother into Indian nationalism. Aurobindo admired Bankim as much for this as for the hope Bankim's work gave of being able to drive out the English language, Krishnadhan's beloved English, from India and install his *mother*-tongue at its place.[44]

---

[42] Mitra, *The Liberator*, p. 37.

[43] *Sri Aurobinder Patra*. Was it the nation which was conceptualized as mother by Aurobindo or was it a still more primal image of the mother which found expression in his concept of India? 'In the unending revolutions of the world, as the wheel of the Eternal turns rightly in the courses, the Infinite Energy, which streams forth from the Eternal and sets the wheel to work. . . . This Infinite Energy is Bhavani. She also is Durga. She is Kali; she is Radha the beloved, she is Lakshmi. She is our mother and creatress of us all. In the present age the mother is manifested as the Mother of Strength.' Aurobindo in *Bhavānī Mandir*, translated by Mitra, *The Liberator*, p. 48.

A good description of Aurobindo's political ideology in the context of his times is in Haridas and Uma Mukherji, *Sri Aurobindo's Political Thought (1893–1908)* (Calcutta: Firma K. L. Mukhopadhyay, 1958).

[44] Aurobindo once proudly said: 'When a Maratha or Gujarati has anything important to say, he says it in English; when a Bengali, he says it in Bengali. . . . English is being steadily driven out of the field. Soon it will only remain to weed it out of our conversation.' *Indu Prakāś*, 23 July 1894. Quoted in Mitra, *The Liberator*, p. 47.

Aurobindo's revolutionary politics ultimately landed him in jail and involved him in a prolonged, dramatic trial on charges of sedition.[45] His year in jail, particularly the time spent in solitary confinement, made a great difference to him spiritually. He practised yoga, read the Gītā and the Upaniṣads, spoke to Vivekananda over the barriers of death and even saw Lord Kṛṣṇa in the jail. Once in a while he broke the monotony by levitating.[46] Even the graces for which he was most thankful were ones he found in jail in 1908: 'the silence' and the 'emptiness'.[47] From then onwards, 'whatever else came, came in the emptiness', and he 'could at any time withdraw from activity into the pure silent peace.'[48]

In May 1909 Aurobindo was acquitted. Sedition in British law was fortunately defined by principles compatible with the philosophy of John Locke, and what in our times, following Isaiah Berlin, we have learnt to call the idea of negative liberty; sedition was not defined under the guidance of the philosophical forebears of Sigmund Freud, or of those of this narrator. Thus, the Oedipal meanings of the private crisis of authority in Krishnadhan's son—through all his political defiance, trial, acquittal and conformity—could remain buried under legal documents. On the other hand, the government was not taken in by Aurobindo's other-worldly rhetoric or by the court order. The threat of re-arrest persisted.[49] Probably, Aurobindo too was not taken in by the liberalism of British law. His mysticism had a pragmatic side and it explicitly included the secular.[50] So, in 1910, on receiving orders 'from above', he

[45] He was later to write an account of his jail days and his trial in elegant, witty Bengali. It was also a brilliant sociological study of British justice in India under stress. Aurobindo Ghose, 'Kārākāhinī', in *Bāṅglā Racanā* (Pondicherry: Sri Aurobindo Ashram, 1977), pp. 257–314.

[46] *On Himself*, p. 68. See also Aurobindo, 'Kārākāhinī'; also Niradbaran, *Sri Aurobindāyan*.

[47] One suspects that he had had them from his earliest years but discovered new, non-threatening meanings for them.

[48] Aurobindo, *On Himself*, p. 89.

[49] Aurobindo had of course expected the acquittal: 'He had been assured from within and knew that he would be acquitted.' *On Himself*, p. 32.

[50] Aurobindo made it clear that his spiritualism had 'nothing to do with ascetic withdrawal or contempt or disgust of secular things.' *On Himself*, p. 430.

moved to Pondicherry, then a French colony in India. There he started a life as a renunciate, to the chagrin of many and yet, in a strange way, following the path traversed by a number of the Bengali terrorists of his time. A small band of followers collected around him in Pondicherry and they lived simply and informally, practising a form of yoga which would free not only India but everybody everywhere. As Aurobindo himself clarified, he now sought *brahmatej*, brāhmaṇic potency obtainable through asceticisms and penances, in the place of *kṣātratej* or martial potency.

This could be the end of the story, but the West had one more decisive intervention to make in Aurobindo's life. In 1914 Mira Paul Richard, at that time an attractive Frenchwoman of thirty-seven, joined Aurobindo, leaving behind her home, husband and children. Aurobindo and Mira had known each other through yoga before they actually met; they had been working together since the dawn of history to carry on the human evolution.[51] (Though their joint work had spanned centuries, they still differed in style: Aurobindo made all his claims part-metaphorically; Mira more literally.[52] Even in occult matters she was more down to earth.) Appropriately enough, she soon took over the organization of the Ashram and was given the title Sri Ma, the Mother, by Aurobindo.

To start with, the group at Pondicherry had been an association of equals, albeit with a charismatic leader. Mira Richard imposed on it formal discipline, a clear hierarchy and ended its *laissez faire* ambience.[53] No pretension of equality was allowed any more;[54] Aurobindo was now the supreme guru and the final key to salvation. Simultaneously, Mira became his new means of communicating with this-worldly others. As

---

[51] Aurobindo, *On Himself*, p. 445. Sri Aurobindo, *The Mother* (Sri Aurobindo Ashram, 1928, republished 1979).

[52] Readers of Bengali might remember Raj Sekhar Bose's savage satire on such idioms in his 'Biriñcibābā', *Kajjali* (Calcutta: M. C. Sarkar and Sons, 1968–9), 10th edition, pp. 1–37.

[53] Aurobindo, *On Himself*, p. 460.

[54] Niradbaran, *Sri Aurobindāyan*; Aurobindo, *On Himself*, p. 460.

he put it, she had 'to come down towards the lower consciousness' because most people sought an authority which was not
too abstract, too distant and too 'severe'.[55] Conceivably for
their benefit, her heavily brocaded figure and even more
heavily made-up face stared down from the walls of the Ashram
as consistently as Aurobindo's.

With the acceptance of Mira as his *śakti* in 1926, Aurobindo
withdrew further into silence and seclusion; only Mira and a
few disciples had close contacts with him and met him regularly.
As for the others, he made four brief appearances a year. The
rest of the time he was kept busy by his yogic attempts to bring
down the supermind to the earth and to produce a new race of
supermen.[56] This seclusion allowed the Mother's control to
become tighter and, after Aurobindo's death, absolute; much
of the open-endedness and imagination of Aurobindo's mysticism was slowly but surely removed by her. The Ashram itself
became, under her powerful presence and efficient guidance,
highly status-conscious, politically conservative and a means
of oppressing the people around. After Aurobindo's death, for
a while it even opposed the decolonization of Pondichery.[57]
Increasingly and inevitably, it acquired the trappings of a well-
organized modern cult and of a church-as-corporation.

The historical reality of a person, however, is never a good
guide to the meanings that are associated with the person.
Thus, for Swarnalata and Krishnadhan's quiet, unprotesting,
long-suffering son, the depth of his relationships with the powerful, committed woman from Europe had an altogether
different meaning. For him, the freed East had at last met the
non-oppressive West symbolized by the Mother. And thence-

[55] Aurobindo, *On Himself*, p. 450.

[56] This idea of the superman had nothing to do with the Nietzschean world
view; Aurobindo's superman was to carry forward the evolution of consciousness
and be more universal in his orientation and more powerful in his ability to change
the world through spiritual attainments.

[57] Claude Alvares, 'Sri Aurobindo, Superman or Supertalk'? *Quest*, January–
February 1975 (93), pp. 9–23, see pp. 10–11. Alvares provides brief but telling
descriptions of the hostility of the local people and Ashram workers to the Ashram.
He however locates the origins of this in Aurobindo's philosophy, which he judges
from the point of view of academic philosophy.

forth his East was incomplete without the Mother's West and his West was partial without her East. The West once separated him from nearness, love and nurture. Now a part of the West had returned to put him in touch with them. 'There is one force only', he declared, 'the Mother's force—or, if you like to put it that way, the Mother is Sri Aurobindo's Force.'[58] And 'if one is open to Sri Aurobindo and not to the Mother it means that one is not really open to Sri Aurobindo.'[59] Gradually, discovering the East in oneself by losing oneself in the East-in-the-West became a transcendent goal and a practical possibility. The last stage of perfection became complete surrender—'when you are completely identified with the Divine Mother and feel yourself to be no longer another and separate being, instrument, servant or worker but truly a child and eternal portion of her consciousness and force.'[60]

Perhaps Aurobindo did after all find a protection against failures of intimacy and nurture, against meaningless silence and emptiness, and against the innermost separations and disjunctions the West had induced in him.

V

It is impossible to read the life of Aurobindo without sensing the 'inner' pain which went with imperialism in India. Much of the pain was inflicted and much of the destruction of his cultural self undertaken within the confines of his family. This further ensured that his suffering passed as education, upbringing or development. It was a total system which young Aurobindo had to confront. Rebellion in such a case was bound to seem hopeless and the 'exotic' alternative he found to it in mysticism was probably the only one available to him. The challenge was to keep the mysticism humane and politically nonconformist. For a long time Aurobindo, within limits, did manage to do that. (It was the organizational edge Mira Richard brought to his spiritualism which turned the language

[58] Aurobindo, *On Himself*, p. 458.   [59] Ibid., p. 458.
[60] Aurobindo, *The Mother*, p. 24.

of spirit into a modern technology of salvation and Aurobindo into India's first modern guru. It was in that guise that Aurobindo spoke of 'intervention in world forces' the way his co-professionals today speak of 'alliance with natural laws'. At this plane, Aurobindo *was* defeated by the West.)

This could be put in another way. If Aurobindo's life story and his spiritualism was a statement of pain it was also an interpersonal withdrawal to protect values which he would have had to give up in the light of conventional reason. And echoing Freud on art, he could have said, only in spiritualism has the omnipotence of thought—and, hence, the political potency and moral vision of the dominated—been retained in our civilization. It was an 'insane', 'irrational' attempt to preserve the ideas of the oneness of man, and of man as a part of an organic universe. In that universe, what a necrophilic war machine did to the Russians at Stalingrad or to the British at Dunkirk, called for intervention by a middle-aged Bengali yogi who had once tried to organize an armed rebellion against the Raj he was now defending. All oppression is one and each man bears his responsibility.

Did Aurobindo symbolize the larger suffering of his society under colonial rule? Did his attempt to speak in a new language parallel his society's attempt to express—and yet protect—its secret awareness of its suffering? No final answers are possible but a few guesses can be made.

First, to protect its self-esteem in the face of defeat, indignity, exploitation and violence, Indian society has indeed evolved a model of autonomy that its victimhood has defined for it. It has evolved a theory of suffering in the form of a set of metaphors which speak through cultural 'absurdities' and moral 'contradictions': the absurdities which spring from an overdone moralism, hiding the pain of protecting values in a world hostile to such values; the contradictions of a victim whose world has been fractured by his need to survive a split authority, part traditional and part imposed. It is the world of a bank-clerk who secretly writes poetry and either hides it from a prosaic world or comically affirms it from the house-top to establish his intellectual superiority. To some, poetry is only poetry and clowns are only clowns and both should be judged as such. To others, poetry—and fooling—could also be a secret defiance, a reaffirmation of the right state of mind in a hard, masculine, anti-poetic world.[61] Defiance need not always be self-conscious. It need not be always backed by the ardent, murderous, moral passions in which the monotheistic faiths, and increasingly the more modern and nationalist versions of Hinduism, specialize.[62]

To the Kiplings and Naipauls such defiance is an obfuscation. Especially as it blurs the lines between the violent and the non-violent, the victorious and the defeated, the past and the present, the material and the non-material. But the victor, insecure in his victory, and the court poet, insecure in his self-

[61] Cf. Theodor W. Adorno's position on the role of culture in society *Minima Moralia*, trans. E. F. N. Jephcott (London: NLB, 1977), pp. 43–4; also Ernst Bloch's position in *On Karl Marx* (New York: Herder and Herder, 1971). This position emerges even more clearly from the chapter on Bloch by Dick Howard in his *The Marxian Legacy* (London: Macmillan, 1977), Chapter 4. Amilcar Cabral places the argument squarely in the context of modern colonialism when he says in his 'National Liberation and Culture', *Return to the Source: Selected Speeches* (New York: Monthly Review Press, 1973), pp. 39–56, pp. 39–40:

'When Goebbels . . . heard culture being discussed, he brought out his revolver. That shows that the Nazis—who were and are the most tragic expression of imperialism and thirst for domination— . . . had a clear idea of the value of culture as a factor of resistance to foreign domination. . . . Whatever may be the material part of this domination, it can be maintained only by the permanent, organized repression of the cultural life of the people concerned.

'The idea for foreign domination, whether imperialist or not, would be to choose:

'—either to liquidate practically all the population of the dominated country, thereby eliminating the possibilities of cultural resistance;

'—or to succeed in imposing itself without damage to the culture of the dominated people—that is to harmonize economic and political domination of these people with their cultural personality.'

The first part of this book is a detailed analysis of this part of the story.

[62] In the Western context the avowed aesthete Oscar Wilde, given both to poetry and to the kind of fooling which in polite society goes by the name of posing, would have understood this. As a poet he sang of things as they were not; as a *poseur* he defied the existent of everyday life. Wilde was a critic not in spite of but because of these. See Richard Ellmann, 'The Critic as Artist as Wilde', *Encounter*, July 1967, pp. 29–37. Wilde was only actualizing the belief of Ernst Bloch that 'banality' is counter-revolutionary.

repression, have both reasons to absolutize relative differences. The defeated, and the poet who, heeding Albert Camus' injunction, sings of the victims of history, have lesser reasons to do so. Thus, what looks like obfuscation and compromise with evil may be seen also as a truer understanding of the oppressors whose suffering and decadence is, for once, taken seriously by their victims, who bear the responsibility of being both the subject and the object of 'history'.[63] What looks like a failure to make cognitive distinctions may in fact be a recognition that the popular modern antonyms are not always the true opposites. This century has shown that in every situation of organized oppression the true antonyms are always the exclusive part versus the inclusive whole—not masculinity versus femininity but either of them versus androgyny, not the past versus the present but either of them versus the timelessness in which the past is the present and the present is the past, not the oppressor versus the oppressed but both of them versus the rationality which turns them into co-victims.

In his own odd way, Aurobindo did try to recognize this on behalf of his culture. To trivialize both the English language and the categories popularized by nineteenth-century Western social criticism, one could perhaps say that in the chaos called India the opposite of thesis is not the antithesis because they exclude each other. The true 'enemy' of the thesis is seen to be in the synthesis because it includes the thesis and ends the latter's reason for being. It is Śaṅkara's Vedānta, carrying the clear impress of Buddhism, which finished Buddhism as a living faith in India, and not either Brāhmaṇic orthodoxy or any state-sponsored anti-Buddhist ideology.[64] Successfully or un-

---

[63] This may sound like a sentence borrowed from George Lukacs. But it is certainly not an attempt to place the sufferer's understanding of the human predicament outside culture and outside time. The formulation is closer to some readings of the works of Antonio Gramsci within the Marxist framework.

[64] By only slightly stretching Madhav Deshpande's analysis, the idea of synthesis here can be made into what Vedānta and Bhaṭṭa Mīmāṁsā call 'a higher order cognition' which can prove false an earlier valid cognition (*paratah aprāmāṇyam* and *svatah prāmāṇyam*). See Deshpande's 'History, Change and Permanence: A Classical Indian Perspective', in Gopal Krishna (ed.), *Contributions to South Asian Studies* 1 (New Delhi: Oxford University Press, 1979), pp. 1–28; particularly p. 3.

successfully, Aurobindo did try to evolve such a response to the West.

Only prolonged victimhood could give depth to such a view of life, even when the view happens to be rooted in ancient wisdom and inherited cosmology. Only the victims of a culture of hyper-masculinity, adulthood, historicism, objectivism, and hypernormality protect themselves by simultaneously conforming to the stereotype of the rulers, by over-stressing those aspects of the self which they share with the powerful, and by protecting in the corner of their heart a secret defiance which reduces to absurdity the victor's concept of the defeated and his unspoken belief that he is morally and culturally superior to his subjects, caught on the wrong side of history.

Almost unwittingly I seem to have come back to Gandhi who was one of the few who successfully articulated in politics the consciousness which had remained untamed by British rule in India. He transformed the debate on Indian hypocrisy into a simultaneous text on British self-doubt. In spite of his occasionally strident moralism, he recognized that once the hegemony of a theory of imperialism without winners and losers was established, imperialism had lost out on cognitive, in addition to ethical, grounds. To the Kiplings this was a threat. They liked to see colonialism as a moral statement on the superiority of some cultures and inferiority of others. For this reason, they were even willing to accept that some had the right to speak of the superiority of Indian culture over the Western. Cultural relativism by itself is not incompatible with imperialism, as long as one culture's categories are backed by political, economic and technological power.

Gandhi queered the pitch at two planes. He admitted that colonialism was a moral issue and took the battle to Kipling's home ground by judging colonialism by Christian values and declaring it to be an absolute evil. At the second plane he made his 'odd' cognitive assessment of the gains and losses from colonialism a part of his critique of modernity and found the British wanting in both ethics and rationality. This threatened the internal legitimacy of the ruling culture by splitting open the private wound of every Kipling and quasi-Kipling to whom rulership was a means of hiding one's moral self in the name of the higher morality of history, in turn seen as an embodiment of human rationality. A naive French imperialist once said in the context of Africa:

I know that I must take pride in my blood. When a superior man ceases to believe himself, he actually ceases to be superior. . . . *When a superior race ceases to believe itself a chosen race, it actually ceases to be a chosen race.*[65]

Gandhi attacked both the cognitive and moral frames of this insecure, fragile sense of chosenness.

In this respect he differed from the other anti-Kiplings to whom colonialism was a moral statement. The final morality to them, too, was 'history' and the immorality of colonialism for them, too, was mitigated by the historical role of colonialism as an instrument of progress. Either through a cultural renaissance set off by the impact of a more vigorous culture (as many of the ninteenth-century social and religious reformers in India and recent modernists in our times have described it) or through the growth of modern capitalism on the way to full-blown liberalism or communism (*à la* the utilitarians and Karl Marx), the modern idea of history has implicitly accepted the cultural superiority—or at least the more advanced cultural state—of the colonizing power.[66] It has thus endorsed

[65] Psichari-Soldier-of-Africa, quoted in Aimé Césaire, *Discourse on Colonialism*, trans. Joan Pinkham (New York: Monthly Review Press, 1977), p. 29. Italics in the original.

[66] Among Indians, elements of such an awareness can be found for example in Rammohun Roy, *The English Works*, vols. I–VI, ed. Kalidas Nag and Debojyoti Burman (Calcutta: Sadharon Brahmo Samaj, 1945–8); Bankimchandra Chatterji, *Racanāvalī*, vols. 1 and 2 (Calcutta: Sahitya Samsad, 1958) (see especially 'Ānandamaṭh', pp. 715–88); Swami Vivekananda, *Prācya o Pāścātya* (Almora: Advaita Ashrama, 1898); and Nirad C. Chaudhuri, *The Autobiography of an Unknown Indian* (London: Macmillan, 1951). Of these, Rammohun Roy and Bankimchandra Chatterji do not fully fit the bill. The former, particularly, lived and worked at a time when one could think of incorporating the ideas of science, history and progress as forces of criticism *within* Indian traditions. He could not visualize an epoch when modernity would take over the world and marginalize all nonmodern cultures as well as the nonmodern West. He was a product of an age which was culturally more self-confident. To a lesser extent, these arguments apply to Chatterji, too.

Cabral has expressed similar sentiments in the context of Africa. See his 'Identity and Dignity in the Context of National Liberation Struggle', *Return to the Source*, pp. 57–69.

one of the major axioms of the colonial theory the Kiplings advanced. As against this, Gandhi reaffirmed an autonomous world view which refused to separate facts from values and refused to see colonialism as an immoral pathway to a valued state of being. Instead of meeting the Western criterion of a true antagonist, he endorsed the non-modern Indian reading of the modern West as one of the many possible life styles which had, unfortunately for both the West and India, become cancerous by virtue of its disproportionate power and spread.

It is this awareness which is the strongest—and the strangest—enemy of modernity in Indian traditions, neither the 'radical' critiques of West nor the aggressive affirmation of Indianness. Modernity, like modern science, could live with everything except an attenuated status and a limited, non-proselytizing social role for it.

The awareness has allowed both insiders and outsiders to define or redefine India and yet refused to force the non-modern Indian to alter his priorities to prove or disprove the cross-sectional ideas of India held by Indians and non-Indians. This is the other way by which the culture has protected its core—by using the dialectic between the continuous attempt by some small groups and persons to define Indianness and large groups to live their life as if such definitions were irrelevant. It is true that traditionally the main instances of Indian creativity, often the main expressions of Indianness, have come from those aspects of Indian consciousness which are nationally and culturally less self-conscious. But it is also true that they can come, less frequently, from the margins of the culture, from among those who can capture in their personal life or in their self-expression something of this cultural tension between self-definition and unselfconsciousness.[67]

[67] I once worked on two Indian scientists and their models of endogenous scientific creativity. One of them, Srinivasa Ramanujan, fell in the first category; the other, Jagadis Chandra Bose, in the second. At the time I wrote my book, my sympathy was mainly with Ramanujan. He seemed to need protection from the modern world. He was less contaminated by that world but, for that very reason, innocent about it while Bose, with his subtle intellectual antennae, could at least manipulate his way through. I am no longer sure of this. Ramanujan was not

The word 'Hindu', T. N. Madan has again recently reminded us, was first used by the Muslims to describe all Indians who were not converted to Islam. Only in recent times have the Hindus begun to describe themselves as Hindus.[68] Thus, the very expression has a built-in contradiction: to use the term Hindu to self-define is to flout the traditional self-definition of the Hindu, and to assert aggressively one's Hinduism is to very nearly deny one's Hinduness. (Rabindranath Tagore's novel *Gorā*, possibly based on the life of the turn-of-the-century nationalist-revolutionary, Brahmabandhab Upadhyay, remains a magisterial study of the nature of this compromise and the underlying cultural and psychological dilemma in the Indian middle-classes.[69]) Fortunately, most Hindus have lived without such self-consciousness for centuries. They certainly did not need an exclusive concept of Hinduism till the nineteenth century when some modernist Hindu religious reformers thought otherwise. They are the ones who tried, in response to the faith of their martial rulers, to indirectly Christianize what they saw as emasculated Hinduism. Appropriately, these modern Hindus saw contemporary Hinduism not as permanently inferior to the Semitic creeds but as a once-great-but-now-fallen religion which had possibilities. So they tried to improve the Hindus and modernize their faith. They sought a sense of community as Hindus and a sense of history as a community.[70]

---

especially vulnerable after all, I found. Nor was Bose particularly inauthentic; the cultural problems he dealt with in his science were real and immediate. And he, too, was vulnerable. As he negotiated his way through the ruthless world of modern science, he had to cope with the hostility which the liminal man always arouses as opposed to the proper alien. Ashis Nandy, *Alternative Sciences: Creativity and Authenticity in Two Indian Scientists* (New Delhi: Allied Publishers, 1980).

[68] 'The Quest for Hinduism', *International Social Science Journal*, 1977, 19(2), pp. 261–78. The psychological counterpart of such open-ended, fluid, cultural self-definition is the 'liquid' reality of the self McKim Marriott speaks about. See his 'The Open Hindu Person and Interpersonal Fluidity', unpublished paper presented at the annual meeting of the Association of Asian Studies, 1980.

[69] Rabindranath Tagore, *Rabindra Racanāvali* (Calcutta: West Bengal Government, 1961), pp. 1–350.

[70] See Part One in this book. See also my 'Psychology of Communalism', *The Times of India*, 19 February 1978; and 'Relearning Secularism', *The Times of India*, 20, 21, and 22 February 1981.

For better or for worse, mainstream Indian culture has learnt to deal with political defeat and instability differently. The sense of community or history which comes from an overlap between religion and nationhood has never been an important constituent of Indian selfhood. The culture has mostly rejected the national self-consciousness which the modern West has tried to foist on it, often through India's own modern spokesmen. Instead, the culture protects itself—against cosmologies which are proselytizing, hegemonistic and committed to some secular or nonsecular theories of cultural evolution—by projecting the idea that the Indian is compromising; he has a fluid self-definition, and he is willing to learn the ways of his civilized brethren unconditionally, provided such learning is profitable. Some cultural traits can be used both as ethnopsychological categories and as protective stereotypes. Thus, like some other cultures caught in an oppressive system, the Indian too does not protest, conforming to the dominant concept of masculine protest, particularly if the cost is too high.[71] But he retains his latent rebelliousness and turns even the standard stereotypes others have of him into effective screens and means of survival. The alternative to Hindu nationalism is the peculiar mix of classical and folk Hinduism and the unselfconscious Hinduism by which most Indians, Hindus as well as non-Hindus, live. It is that liminality which Kipling resented. It is that liminality on which the greatest of Indian social and political leaders built their self-definition as Indians over the last two centuries.[72]

No better example can be given than that of the 'comic' and 'absurd' mix of the folksy and the canonical, and of the 'hypocritical' mix of effective protest and the 'minimum gesture of protest' in the political style of Gandhi, a man sometimes compared to Charles Chaplin and Micky Mouse less seriously than one wishes. General Jan H. Smuts (1870–1950), South

[71] Cf. E. D. Genovese, *Roll, Jordan, Roll: The World the Slaves Made* (New York: Pantheon, 1970); Frantz Fanon, *The Wretched of the Earth.*

[72] These leaders have partially coped with the problem of non-critical traditions in India which Pratima Bowes seems to pose in her *The Hindu Intellectual Tradition* (New Delhi: Allied Publishers, 1977).

African prime minister and one of Gandhi's staunchest enemies and admiring friends, unwittingly admitted the power of this mix in a tired, exasperated comment on Gandhi's departure from South Africa. 'The saint has left our shores', he said, 'I sincerely hope for ever.' And here is Richard Lannoy's description of the Salt March, built on snippets garnered from a number of sources. I hope it provides a clue to the exasperation of both Smuts and his brain-children in modern India with a man and a method which rejected not merely *kṣātratej* but also, it seems, *brahmatej*:

The Salt March makes its point through richly tragi-comic incident(s) . . .

Gandhi marches for twenty-four days from his *ashram* in Ahmedabad to Dandi, 241 miles distant on the seashore, there to pick up salt in defiance of the Salt Laws imposed with crushing effect on the Indian peasant by the British Raj. After defying the laws *he withdraws from the action.* . . .

Behind the Salt March lie years of patient preparation. . . . The Satyagrahis are taught how to obtain strength through perfect weakness, or, if one likes, *how to do nothing.* . . . In a tropical climate salt is a staple food; Gandhi had already renounced the eating of salt for six years. In advance, he announces his intention to break the law himself by writing to his 'Dear friend' the Viceroy of India, Lord Irwin. . . .

The image of Gandhi marching in a loin-cloth to the seashore with a motley band of seventy-eight workers set on picking up a pinch of salt is deceptively anachronistic, even in 1930. The march was to last sufficient time for the eyes of India and the world to be riveted on the frail old man of sixty-one plodding on under a merciless March sun. . . . 'On the Salt March he fully entered the world of the newsreel and documentary. Henceforth we have many glimpses of him flickering in black and white, a brisk, mobile figure, with odd but illuminating moments of likeness to Charlie Chaplin' (Ashe). As Gandhi Marched, behind him 'the administration was silently crumbling as three hundred and ninety village headmen resigned their posts' (Ashe).

. . . 'And there was Gandhi, walking along, with his friends round him, it was a sort of terrific anti-climax. There was no cheering, no great shouts of delight, and no sort of stately procession at all, it was all rather, in a sense rather farcical . . . there I was, seeing history happen in a strange anti-climax way: something completely un-European and yet very, very moving' (Bolton).

When they reached Dandi they camped for seven days, eating parched grain, half an ounce of fat, and two ounces of sugar daily. On 6 April Gandhi rose at dawn, took his bath in the sea, and then walked over to the natural salt deposits. Photographers at the ready, he picked up a treasonable pinch of salt and handed it to a person standing at his side. Sarojini Naidu cried out, 'Hail deliverer!' and then he went back to his work.

The news flashed round the world and within days India was in turmoil; millions were preparing salt in every corner of the land. Vast demonstrations were held in every large city in the country, from Karachi to Madras. Women in purdah mounted demonstrations in the streets. Like automata, the British administration responded with blind and incoherent action of extreme violence. The army and police moved as if hypnotized into a response from which all meaning had vanished. Indians were beaten, kicked in the groin, bitten in the fingers, and fired on by vindictive constables. They were charged by cavalry until they lay on the ground at the horses' feet. . . . Between 60,000 and 100,000 non-violent resistors went to jail. Save for one small incident at Chittagong, Bengal, no Indian struck a violent blow. Gandhi was arrested after midnight sleeping under a tree in camp near Dandi and sent to jail. On his release eight months later he concluded the Gandhi–Irwin pact, after which the government abandoned its repressive measures and released political prisoners. This was the occasion when . . . Nehru wept.

. . . Louis Fischer concludes his account of the Salt March with a crisp comment: 'India was now free. Technically, legally, nothing had changed.'[73]

At some plane, Lannoy *has* caught the spirit of the 'halting, stop-go' style of creative politics in India:

Everything is for ever going wrong, in Satyagraha as in the myths. Yet, . . . one cannot help drawing the conclusion that Gandhian Satyagraha is peculiarly well suited to permit the transformation of setbacks into what Zimmer describes as 'miraculous development', jolting the movement from crisis to crisis. Zimmer ascribes this familiar 'muddling through' in the Puranic myths to insight into the essential

[73] Richard Lannoy, *The Speaking Tree*, pp. 400–7; Geoffrey Ashe, *Gandhi: A Study in Revolution* (London: Heinemann, 1968), p. 286; Glorney Bolton in Francis Watson and Maurice Brown (eds.), *Talking of Gandhiji* (London: Longmans, Green, 1957), pp. 58–9. Italics in original.

nature of the contending forces. . . . Ultimately, this rests on . . . acceptance of suffering. . . . Under certain Indian conditions this 'passivity' is probably more effective. . . .[74]

Let me sum up in the words of an English character from *A Passage to India* who says, perhaps influenced by her experience in India, 'there are many kinds of failure, some of which succeed.'

The differentia of Indian culture has often been sought by social analysts, including this writer, in the uniqueness of certain cultural themes or in their configuration. This is not a false trail, but it does lead to some half-truths. One of them is the clear line drawn, on behalf of the Indian, between the past and the present, the native and the exogenous, and the Hindu and the non-Hindu. But, as I have suggested, the West that is aggressive is sometimes inside; the earnest, self-declared native, too, is often an exogenous category, and the Hindu who announces himself so, is not that Hindu after all. Probably the uniqueness of Indian culture lies not so much in a unique ideology as in the society's traditional ability to live with cultural ambiguities and to use them to build psychological and even metaphysical defences against cultural invasions. Probably, the culture itself demands that a certain permeability of boundaries be maintained in one's self-image and that the self be not defined too tightly or separated mechanically from the not-self. This is the other side of the strategy of survival—the clue to India's post-colonial world view—which I have discussed above.

I remember Ivan Illich once recounting how a group of fifteenth-century Aztec priests who, herded together as sorcerers by their Spanish conquerors, said in response to a Christian sermon that if as alleged the Aztec gods were dead, they too would rather die. After this last act of defiance, the priests were dutifully thrown to the war dogs. I suspect I know how a group of Brāhmaṇ priests would have behaved under the same circumstances. All of them would have embraced Christianity and

[74] Lannoy, *The Speaking Tree*, pp. 404–5.

some of them would have even co-authored an elegant *prasasti*
to praise the alien rulers and their gods. Not that they would
have become good Christians overnight. Most probably their
faith in Hinduism would have remained unshaken and their
Christianity would have looked after a while dangerously like
a variation on Hinduism. But under the principle of *āpaddharma*,
or the way of life under perilous conditions, and the principle of
oneness of every being—the metaphysical correlate of what a
well-intentioned Freudian modernist has called projective ex-
traversion born of extreme narcissism[75]—they would have felt
perfectly justified in bowing down to alien gods and in overtly
renouncing their culture and their past. The Hindus have traditionally felt burdened with the responsibility of protecting their
civilization not by being self-conscious, but by securing a
mythopoetic understanding—and thus neutralizing—the missionary zeal of their conquerors. What looks like Westernization
is often only a means of domesticating the West, sometimes by
reducing the West to the level of the comic and the trivial. As
the Hindu Purāṇas repeatedly seem to suggest, blind, straight
courage is all right for individual piety and immortality, not
for ensuring collective survival.[76] And there is also perhaps the
feeling, legitimized by more canonical texts, that the Dionysian
can be internalized and then contained by the wise. It need not
be always fought as an outside force.

Yastu sarvāṇi bhūtāni ātmanyevānupaśyati
Sarvabhūteṣu cātmānam tato na vijugupsate[77]

At a more mundane plane, our hypothetical Brāhmaṇs would
be splitting their personalities. To them, the conversion and

---

[75] Philip Spratt, *Hindu Culture and Personality* (Bombay: Manaktalas, 1966).

[76] For instance, it is possible to read the political and social choices of Kṛṣṇa
in the Mahābhārata entirely along these lines. Probably the more significant clue
is the traditional responsibility for sustenance and protection of the Brāhmaṇs and
the responsibility for disjunctive, normative creativity given to renunciators like
Aurobindo. On this see Louis Dumont, *Homo Hierarchicus* (London: Weidenfeld
and Nicolson, 1970).

[77] 'He who sees every being in his own self and sees himself in every other being,
he, because of this vision, abhors nothing.' 'Īsopaniṣad', in Atulchandra Sen (ed.),
Upaniṣad (Calcutta: Haraf, 1972), pp. 130–55; see especially p. 138.

the humiliation would be happening to a self which is already seen and felt as some*body* else or as somebody else's. This is a self from whom one is already somewhat abstracted and alienated. Such splitting of one's self, to protect one's sanity and to ensure survival, makes the subject an object to himself and disaffiliates the violence and the humiliation he suffers from the 'essential constituent' of his self.[78] It is an attempt to survive by inducing in oneself a psychosomatic state which would render one's immediate context partly dreamlike or unreal. Because, 'in order to live and stay human, the survivor must be in the world but not of it.'[79] (In the final analysis, this has been one of the major psychological responses of Indian spiritualism to the West, whatever be its metaphysical content. Using the ancient distinction between what could be called the existential consciousness or *ātman* and the attribute consciousness, which modern psychologists mainly study, most schools of Indian spiritualism give meaning to a controlled inner schism which, instead of threatening mental health, contributes to a peculiar robust realism. It helps one, to use Ananda Coomaraswamy's language in an altogether different sense, to master fate and transcend necessity and to 'become the Spectator of all time and all things'.[80]) For all we know, the Indian's alleged weak grasp on reality, his weak ego, his easy transference to political authorities and his vague presence in social situations—howsoever deeply rooted in traditional child rearing they may

[78] Confronting a concentration camp for the first time, psychiatrist Elie Cohen found himself resorting to a similar splitting. See his *Human Behaviour in the Concentration Camp*, trans. M. H. Braaksma (New York: Norton, 1953), p. 116, quoted in Terence Des Pres, *The Survivor: An Anatomy of Life in the Death Camp* (New York: Oxford University Press, 1976), p. 82. The idea of the 'essential constituent of the self' is Erving Goffman's. It has meanings similar to the more loosely defined idea of the core of Indianness used in this analysis. See Goffman's *Asylums: Essays on the Social Situation of Mental Patients and Other Inmates* (Chicago: Aldine, 1962), p. 319. Goffman calls this entire process 'secondary adjustment'. It involves the rejection of the self imposed by a total institution or situation.

[79] Des Pres, *The Survivor*, p. 99.

[80] Ananda K. Coomaraswamy, 'On the Indian and Traditional Psychology, or Rather Pneumatology', *Selected Papers*, vol. 2: *Metaphysics*, ed. Roger Lipsey (Princeton: Princeton University Press, 1977) pp. 333–78, see especially pp. 365, 377.

seem to be—are also the inescapable logic of a culture ex-
periencing problems of survival over generations. To fit the
logic to the experience of another victim at another time, these
'personality failures' of the Indian could be another form of
developed vigilance, or sharpened instinct or faster reaction to
man-made suffering.[81] They come not from 'a fundamental
submissiveness to authority' which breaks through some of
Kipling's more shameless apologia for the Empire, but from a
certain talent for and faith in life.[82] To borrow a picturesque
image from Kipling's account of his own oppressed childhood
in England, some people are fated to live long stretches of time
like hunted animals and to keep their senses perpetually on the
alert to escape from the toils of the hunters.[83]

Ever since the modern West's encounter with the non-
Western world, the response of the Aztec priets has seemed to
the Westernized world the paragon of courage and cultural
pride; the hypothetical response of the Brāhmaṇ priests hypocritical and cowardly. But the question remains why every
imperialist observer of the Indian society has loved India's
martial races and hated and felt threatened by the rest of
India's 'effeminate' men willing to compromise with their
victors? What is it in the latter that has aroused such anti-
pathy? Why should they matter so much to the conquerers of
India if they are so trivial? Why could they so effortlessly become the antonyms of their rulers? Why have so many modern
Indians shared this imperialist estimation? Why have they felt
proud of those who fought out and lost, and not of those who
lost out and fought?

At one plane the answer is simple. The Aztec priests after
their last act of courage die and they leave the stage free for
those who kill them and then sing their praise; the unheroic
Indian response ensures that part of the stage always remains

---

[81] Halina Birenbaum, *Hope is the Last to Die*, trans. David Welsh (New York:
Twayne, 1971), p. 103, quoted in Des Pres, *The Survivor*, p. 87.

[82] Cf. Gita Sereny, *Into That Darkness* (New York: McGraw-Hill, 1974), p. 183.

[83] *Stalky's Reminiscences* (London, 1928), pp. 30–1, quoted in Edmund Wilson,
'The Kipling that Nobody Read', p. 22.

occupied by the 'cowardly' and the 'compromising' who may at some opportune moment assert their presence. And then, there is the added advantage that the Aztec priests set a good precedent for—and endorsed the world view of—the lower classes of the colonial societies which have to serve as the foot-soldiers of colonialism. There is, thus, a vested interest in the simple courage of the Aztec priests.

But another answer to the question can also be given. It is that the average Indian has always lived with the awareness and possiblity of long-term suffering, always seen himself as protecting his deepest faith with the passive, 'feminine' cunning of the weak and the victimized, and surviving outer pressures by refusing to overplay his sense of autonomy and self-respect. At his heroic best, he is a satyagrahi, one who forges a partly-coercive weapon called satyagraha out of what Lannoy calls 'perfect weakness'. In his non-heroic ordinariness, he is the archetypal survivor. Seemingly he makes all-round compromises, but he refuses to be psychologically swamped, co-opted or penetrated. Defeat, his response seems to say, is a disaster and so are the imposed ways of the victor. But worse is the loss of one's 'soul' and the internalization of one's victor, because it forces one to fight the victor according to the victor's values, within his model of dissent. Better to be a comical dissenter than to be a powerful, serious but acceptable opponent.[84] Better to be a hated enemy, declared unworthy of any respect whatsoever, than to be a proper opponent, constantly making 'primary adjustments' to the system.[85]

In order to truly live, the inviolable core of Indianness seems to affirm, it might be sometimes better to be dead in somebody else's eyes, so as to be alive for one's own self. In order to accept oneself, one must learn to hold in trust 'weaknesses' to which

---

[84] It is interesting that organized Islam in India has always feared losing its identity. The dominant ideology of Islam in India has always been confident that it could hold its own against Hinduism in statecraft and in martial prowess; it has always feared being overwhelmed or swamped by the slow, soporific sedativity of everyday Hinduism. This has never been the fear of folk Islam because it shares the world view of folk Hinduism to a great extent.

[85] Goffman, *Asylums*.

a violent, culturally barren and politically bankrupt world
some day may have to return.

VI

> . . . national liberation is necessarily an act of *culture*.
>
> Amilcar Cabral[86]

> In the animal kingdom, the rule is, eat or be eaten; in the human
> kingdom, define or be defined.
>
> Thomas Szasz[87]

Those who have found the foregoing a loose-ended, old-style
narrative may read the postscript as the moral of the story.

I have examined, under different rubrics, four sets of polarities which have informed most discourses on the East and the
West in colonial and post-colonial times. These polarities are:
the universal versus the parochial, the material (or the realistic)
versus the spiritual (or the unrealistic), the achieving (or the
performing) versus the non-achieving (or the non-performing),
and the sane versus the insane.[88] I have also touched upon a
fifth set which cuts across these four: a self-conscious, well-
defined Indianness versus a fluid open self-definition. At one
plane, I have tried to show that the two ends of these polarities
meet if the central problem is coping with—or resistance to—

[86] Cabral, 'National Liberation and Culture', p. 43. Italics in the original.
[87] Thomas S. Szasz, *The Second Sin* (London: Routledge and Kegan Paul, 1974),
p. 20.
[88] The last two polarities may not be as disparate if we remember Michel
Foucault's formulation that the confinement of the insane and the confinement of
the criminal were both related to the confinement of the idle, that is of those who
defied the oppression of modern industrial work. See *Madness and Civilization: A
History of Insanity in the Age of Reason*, trans. Richard Howard (London: Tavistock,
1971), Chapter 2; and *Discipline and Punish*, trans. Alan Sheridan (Harmondsworth:
Penguin, 1978), particularly Part 3. Szasz writes in *The Second Sin*, p. 89:
'Among persons categorized as mentally ill, there are two radically different
types which are systematically undifferentiated by psychiatrists and hence confused by them. One is composed of the inadequate, unskilled, lazy, or stupid; in
short, the unfit (however relative this term might be). The other of the protestors,
the revolutionaries, those on strike against their relatives or society; in short, the
unwilling.
'Because they do not differentiate between these two groups, psychiatrists often
attribute unfitness to unwillingness, and unwillingness to unfitness.'

oppression and not the scholarly understanding of a civilization. At another plane, I have tried to show that the parochial,
the spiritual, the non-performing and the insane can sometimes
turn out to be better versions of the universal, the realistic, the
efficient and the sane.

At neither of the planes, however, have I tried to reverse the
standard stereotypes to create a neo-romantic ideology of the
irrational, the mythic or the renunciatory. Nor have I tried to
legitimize the populist imagery of an all-knowing common man.
My concerns here are unheroic rather than heroic and empirical rather than philosophical. The argument is that when
psychological and cultural survival is at stake, polarities such
as the ones discussed here do break down and become partly
irrelevant, and the directness of the experience of suffering and
spontaneous resistance to it come through at all planes. When
this happens, there emerges in the victim of a system a vague
awareness of the larger whole which transcends the system's
analytic categories and/or stands them on their head. Thus, the
victim may become aware that, under oppression, the parochial
could protect some forms of universalism more successfully than
does conventional universalism; that the spiritualism of the
weak may articulate or keep alive the values of a non-oppressive
world better than the ultra-materialism of those who live in
vision-less worlds; and that the non-achieving and the insane
may often have a higher chance of achieving their civilizational
goal of freedom and autonomy without mortgaging their
sanity. I imply that these paradoxes are inevitable because the
dominant idea of rationality is the first strand of consciousness
to be co-opted by any successful structure of institutionalized
oppression. When such co-optation has taken place, resistance
as well as survival demands some access to the larger whole,
howsoever self-defeating that process may seem in the light of
conventional reason and day-to-day politics. This, I suspect,
is another way of restating the ancient wisdom—which for some
cultures is also an everyday truism—that knowledge without
ethics is not so much bad ethics as inferior knowledge.

Index